AGE OF ANXIETY

CONSTANTINE TSOUCALAS

AGE OF ANXIETY

Translated by
Alex Stavrakas

ERIS

An imprint of Urtext
Unit 6 53 Beacon Road
London SE13 6ED, UK

Copyright © Constantine Tsoucalas, 2010
Translation © Alex Stavrakas, 2018

Originally published in Greece by Kastaniotis in 2010
This first English edition published by Eris in 2018

Printed and bound in Great Britain

ISBN 978-1-912475-14-8

eris.press

CONTENTS

1

IDENTITY
Takes its Place on the Political Stage

Panta rhei. Everything flows—in nature, in society, in our minds. Our thoughts, like living organisms, are in a state of constant flux. They succumb to external pressures and obey unknown laws, they move relentlessly, accelerating and slowing down, advancing and retreating, attempting sudden leaps along a route that has neither direction nor end. The historical selection of ideas resembles the natural selection of species: the resilience of meanings in this march toward an unknown destination is unpredictable, and the dust of intellectual progress that is scattered by the relentless survival struggle will only retrospectively appear settled. What exists tends to be reproduced wholesale, while newcomers must overcome the inertia of social dynamics and the reflexes that existing semantic orders trigger. Worldviews aren't deposed voluntarily. In a state of vigilant wakefulness, established ideas tend to defend themselves against insidious intruders, whereas new ones, like spermatozoa, look for eggs to fertilise.

But wakefulness itself isn't something new: societies have always devised ways of handling the 'new gods'. What has changed is the way novelty is perceived: intuitions are ever more frequently undermined, ideological convictions weakened, certainties readily abandoned, and entire value systems are deconstructed and reassembled anew overnight. Misreading Arthur Rimbaud ("we must at all costs remain absolutely modern"), zealots of unrestrained modernisation have fetishised newness: conceptual constructs seem finally rid of the compulsion to eternally repeat the same over and over; new ideas, regardless of their actual merit, are perceived *ipso jure* superior to old ones; even language can't tame the forces of change; instead, it is subordinated to them. What's more, the terms that grant access to the valid-as-true have been accorded their own unique political correctness.

Talk of identity and difference must, then, take into account three facts: one, the discourse's merciless intrusion into an already disturbed setting; two, the eagerness with which it is being imposed; and, three, the effortlessness with which it seems to be displacing the established order. *Difference*, suddenly and in stark contrast with the patterns that heretofore designated the political field, is no longer just a natural state, but a crucial claim. The unprecedented clamour of demands for recognition, talk of the individual's right to difference, and issues surrounding multiculturalism all herald an ideological turn with unpredictable consequences. When difference and multiculturalism take the place of homogeneity and unitarity, the very coordinates of social organisation are at stake.

This means that these notions at the core of the individual's relation to the social collective will migrate to the centre of socio-political enquiry. Bearers of institutionalised and incontestable personal rights, individuals will have to embrace the additional task of determining their identity and carving out their own special otherness. Even if these developments do not immediately register as explicit regulatory adjustments, the shift in attitude is itself telling of a new era. Things are unfolding as if the now-distant existential uncertainty of the untroubled modern socio-political thought is forced to give way to an externally dictated and standardised conformity about primordial alterity. The already unconvincing answers to the question *Who am I?* are for the first time in recent history elevated to objects of systemic control. Identity is politicised.

This book looks at the historical conditions of this ideological remodelling. It focuses on the current political discourse that revolves around identity and difference, a discourse that seems entirely symptomatic of our times. Regardless of complex ethical parameters, underlying this ostensibly pathological obsession with individuality and freedom of choice, with collective identity, recognition[1], and with difference[2] is a widespread confusion caused by radical shifts in the historical function of social collectives and of the state. It doesn't seem at all surprising that the sudden outburst of discussion about identities is gaining ground at a time when, one, the ideological cohesion and conceptual wholesomeness of liberal societies is in decline; and when, two, conventional understandings of the relation between individual and society, national and supranational, political and cultural, and, generally, between the individual and its social surrounding are all undergoing sweeping reforms. Seen in this light, the right to difference seems inextricably tied to a semantic redefinition of the conditions of differentiation within the social setting. If representations of the person's place in the world and the terms used for understanding society as a solid and incontestable cultural unity are being reconsidered, the same will happen to the terms concerning human self-knowledge. And, if Gadamer was right when he wrote that "more than anything, understanding constitutes being and produces history"[3], then we might indeed be at a turning point. Although it remains impossible to deduce any intention as such behind a historical happening that stubbornly refuses to end, we have every reason to believe—hope, even—that the period we are going through is transitional.

One thing is certain: as far as the terms that we use for understanding ourselves and society are concerned, the break with the recent past is by all means radical. Around the world, delineated and conceptually airtight socio-cultural schemes have been replaced by increasingly open, precarious, unruly even, social formations. The cohesion, stability, and self-sufficiency of grand narratives have been irrevocably compromised. Its political context aside, Thatcher's emblematic catchphrase, "There is no such thing as society: there are individual men and women", seems to capture the essence of an age when singular, imaginarily invested, and objectively definable collectives that sustained individuals have been replaced by a vitiating cluster of *alternatives*. Traditional forms of nostalgia and the societies that induced them will never be the same again. Solid and shared symbolic structures have found themselves knee-deep in boundless individualism, saturated with vague anti-statist sentiment, and corroded by the overabundance of irreconcilable signals, symbols, and choices, and can thus no longer function as the palpable reproductive hubs of meaning they once were.[4] Those ideological bonding agents which guaranteed cultural homogeneity and regulatory independence in societies have been incapacitated, debilitated, and, worse, privatised. We are drifting within a constellation of universal haziness, increased vagueness, and semantic disorder. It has become harder to gauge the objective historical potency of reality whilst remaining capable of deciphering the meanings and limits of information.[5] Even if we want to change the world, we have no idea how, or where to start, or what tools to use, or, even, what it is that we want to change.

To make matters worse, this lack of focus has distorted the psychological parameters of socialisation. It has weakened the reassuring sense of belonging to a finite, stable, and coherent social whole. Fewer people than ever seek to satisfy their practical or existential needs as members of some collective entity. Fewer, still, find comfort in the embrace of a multitude that allows them to express their impulses and manage—even possibly control—their inborn panics.[6] Although people are still free not to overestimate the effectiveness of their personal desires and acts[7] and whilst remaining cautious of the freedoms available to them[8], even so, they are expected to toil in solitude to gain their own values and their own meanings, to understand the world and name its contents using their own terms, to choose their own course of action, and to solve their own problems, privately. The range of personal choice has expanded, offering abundant and often contradictory messages outside common networks of meanings and symbols.[9] This type of freedom owes its appeal to the fact that, like the object of faith, it can be neither proven nor refuted[10], which explains why it is being offered as both a universal cure *and* a placebo.[11] But, like most conventional wisdoms, it too has proven to be spectacularly false: the expansion of liberties hasn't delivered the dawn of a new age of reason we were promised. Our current convictions are neither more rational nor less irrational than the ones they deposed. On the contrary: disenchantment never seemed a more distant feat.[12]

2

The FUTURE *Appears*

This book is divided in five parts. It begins with the
claim that any understanding of identities and differences can *only* be socio-historical. The meaning
and function of words is intrinsically bound to the
particular conceptual schemes within which these
words emerge. In this sense, the unfolding of social
representations of identity must be placed inside a
wider range of ideas that originated in eighteenth-
century European thought. Whether legitimate
children or bastards of the Enlightenment, we are
all still clinging to its apron strings. Openly or not,
we agree that all statements—including those that
vainly try to elucidate the issue of who we are—must
be articulated and substantiated rationally, and that
they must comply with the fundamental, universal,
and inalienable value of liberty.[1] Before we can even
pose a question, we must think and speak as rational
and free agents.

This in itself was a historic break with the past.
Ideas about the organisation and politics of society,
about the meaning of selfhood and otherness,

about being human, and about individual and collective identities were henceforth uncoupled (gradually and, when necessary, forcibly) from traditional irrational and illiberal (or pre-liberal) religious and ethnic origins. This made central again the primordial question of signalling the first-person plural, *We*. Future societies made up of free individuals would not be able to rely—at least not exclusively—on divine orders, straightforward and obvious cohabitation rules, or the whimsical expectations of the perennially oppressive ruling classes any more so than on the Aristotelian desire to live together. What we refer to as *public*, and its relation to the parts that inhabit and constitute it, would have to be justified and rationalised based on coherent and consistent principles.

As a result, those distinctly modern procedures that are responsible for generating and solidifying a nonintuitive ontological meaning for societies (and, for that matter, *all* collective entities) were born.[2] Free and rational individuals were expected to join together and socialise as if convinced of both the necessity and the rationality of the whole, even if they didn't believe in it. The *ratio essendi* of societies and groups, unnatural and forced as it is[3], became the object of a wider theoretical enquiry, and the issue of establishing and rationalising organised authority as a lawful and rational community of free people was suddenly inescapable.

In this sense, the predominance of Rousseau's rational and cohesive contractual societies, Herder's historically rigid and necessary *Volksgeist*, and Hegel's understanding of the state as the embodiment of the transcendental spirit, are all parts of the same historical and logical framework. Societies, being by definition contractual, national, and rational, must be perceived as both concrete and uniform closed political and cultural orders[4] that can be legitimised as necessary and holistically constituted conceptual constructs.[5] Under these conditions, notions surrounding the relationship of the individual with society would be placed at the centre of a new discourse that would fulfil the emerging functions, address the priorities of, and satisfy the notional prerequisites for the establishment of contemporary powers. As a result, contractual formations, enduring national cultures, and exclusive collective identities would be established within a common historical process. It looked as if the circle could close; maybe, even, be squared.

But, unsurprisingly, history had other plans. The prevalence of state nationalism established new threats to the dominant ideological, political, and conceptual harmony. From a very early stage, national and religious minorities challenged the authority of insulated national symbolic integrations. The creation of nation-state entities led to a spontaneous proliferation and hardening of unprecedented geopolitical and ideological reactions and tensions. The centripetal national identities destined to bring about the ultimate state came face-to-face with centrifugal minorities that threatened them anew with doctrinal imbalance and disorder.

Once again, it becomes clear that the backdrop against which conflicting powers are organised could not self-propagate as if rid of the historical rust that corrodes it. With history lurking ghostly in the wings, the imaginary of the political aspect of social uniformity, stubbornly impervious to rationalising constructs, is practically impossible to settle once and for all. In this sense, the proliferation of national minorities constitutes *by itself* a resistance to the idea of a nation. And for this very reason, minorities seem to always rise from their ashes like a mythical Phoenix, feeding off the scraps of new orders, and exposing them to new threats and challenges.

Chapter 4 looks at changes occurring in today's world. In our so-called *globalised* world, the increasing transnational mobility of people, the opening up of borders, and the widespread dominance of capitalist forms of social organisation have engendered decisive displacements in the terms used for understanding collective identity.[6] Against these erratic, fluctuating, hybrid social embodiments, the dominant discourse will need to venture into unfamiliar interpretive territory if it wants to imagine anew its structural prescriptions. The rigorous distinction between private and public spheres will be relativised; the relationship between political and financial powers will be redesigned; and the strict separation of state and society will be weakened. Since traditionally solid and recognisable national cultures can no longer pose as unquestionable, over-arching, and inalienable collective values, power structures will have to invent increasingly imaginative ways to handle unpredictability and uncertainty, contain randomness, and deal with precariousness and impermanence. Naturally, the conditions for wedding reality's functional and organisational aspects to its symbolic substance must shift. The struggle against entropic forces will take place elsewhere; the need for social reproduction will move in new directions; and the demand for cohesion will be invested with a new ideological and political terminology. The forms of signalling and reproducing shared values and the organised social being will never be the same.

The following chapter (Chapter 5) addresses some of the ideological consequences of these new forms of socio-political instability. Indeed, the debasement of the concept of nation-state and the rise of individual cultural self-determination seem to go hand in hand with the triumph and glorification of rampant self-centredness, with the end of public accountability, and with the privatisation of responsibility for one's life. It's not a coincidence that although many traditional forms of socialisation (especially education) have remained in the hands of nation-states, their objective is drifting farther away from the original mission of instilling and cultivating common values and ideals (universal or local) into members of society. In the coming years, the main duty of ideological mechanisms will be breeding autonomously competitive, professionally potent, voluntarily acquiescent, and ungrudgingly domesticated individuals. The demand for a collectively advancing symbolic harmony and cohesion will be replaced by the demand for the best possible instrumental acclimation of each person *separately* to a wider, ungovernable, open environment. The disenthralment of societies from specificity means people will become static notional matrices.

Chapter 6 deals with the specific consequences of these new models of socialisation on the structure and function of mechanisms responsible for the reproduction of social relations, particularly in the case of education. The deregulation of welfare states and the enfeeblement of labour welfare contributed massively to the intensification of a global and at the same time endemic survival uncertainty which not only overdetermines workplace conditions, but also influences socialisation. For instance, instead of the now-neglected demand for guaranteed employment within a consistently stratified world, we get the fanciful idea of lifelong learning which ensures that competitive individuals can constantly restock their skills and cognitive reserve to find a place within a workforce that appears to be naturally volatile. Socialisation, then, becomes the process of ingraining individualistic industrial vigour that an unpredictably developing job market might only retrospectively recognise, and possibly reward. And in this sense, people are appointed not only in charge of, but also accountable for, their own professional future. Their constantly and freely available personality is their only inalienable property. Self-differentiation has ceased being an ordinary and dispassionate cultural fact; as the object of a universal prescription, it has been elevated to a tactical priority.

Finally, Chapter 7 reveals the unforeseen political aspects of those transformations. Idiosyncratic cultural emancipation cannot be seen separately from changes in the methods and objectives of power—it goes hand in hand with the establishment of an entire network of social relationships where the whole renounces not only its pastoral duties but also its symbolic jurisdiction. Everything seems to be taking place as if the right to difference and the demand for individual cultural self-determination are solutions to a problem: a social, ideological, and political problem that happens to coincide with the decline of all the mechanisms responsible for protecting and caring after people who have no options except those which they *deserve*. In our contemporary risk societies[7], the main objective of socialisation seems to be privatising liability and implementing a choice-based versatility vis-à-vis the challenges posed by ever-changing circumstances and lurking dangers.

Power strategies are shifting. People are not taught to think and function as members of an imaginarily firm community. Instead, they are forced to live and act as individuals responsible for their own socialisation. From the moment that the state is relieved of the duty to treat its immaculate symbolic unity as a matter of prime concern, the propagation and reproduction of free, varying, uncertain, and potentially composite identities not only poses no threat to it but, on the contrary, it sits perfectly with its systemic fluctuations. In this sense, the widespread success of the notion of personal responsibility is maybe nothing more than an ideological escape that a system of social powers attempts when it no longer needs to enforce any demanding and unpleasant excesses. The promise of the *end of history* is concomitant with the end of moral deliberation for politics.

3

The New
ALCHEMY

"I am infinite and inexhaustible", said Sartre[1]; Paul Valéry added, "I was born several and I died one"[2]. This is not just a philosophical exercise: everyday life shows that the first-person singular, *I*, is not experienced as constant and unchangeable[3], nor is it perceived as a specific transhistorical universalium.[4] Internal cohesion of conscience is assembled gradually through an open-ended process. Identity cannot be treated as an indistinguishable natural quality.[5] Curiously[6], even if the feeling of some narrative continuity and cohesion is necessary, the shaping of self-conscience is always related to the conditions of internalising the relationship of each person *with others*.[7] Perhaps this fact is the essential component of self-reflexivity that the Cartesian "I think, therefore I am" tried to bypass. Although (to paraphrase Freud) while what we call *I* constitutes a necessary formation around which the totality of intellectual activities are organised, the *meaning* of this formation remains inescapably trapped inside specific social contexts.

Something much more intricate is at work in what concerns the conditions of understanding collective identity—whether by *collective* we mean a group, or society as a whole. Even if the construction of *we* is itself no more contingent, complex, or indirect than the construction of *I*, it still adheres to the necessarily intricate, externally imposed, and unpredictable restrictions of a perpetually unfolding historical happening. The understanding of first-person plural must appear cognitively consistent with the prescriptions relevant to the first-person singular. Additionally, from the moment that it appears anchored to the labyrinthine collective self-reflexivity, allusions to *us* are also over-determined by history.

Regardless of epistemological prescriptions and the psychological and social realities they express, historical notions that refer to a constant self or social formation amount to semantic—even imaginary—constructs necessarily charged with the historicity of cultures within which they emerge.[8] This is what Deleuze and Guattari meant when, inspired by Hume[9], they wrote that the "I is a habit"[10]. In addition to semantic structures, cultures also construct their own ideas and conceptual schemes harmoniously aligned with prevalent interpretations of the *I* and *we*. In this regard, individuals couldn't be considered capable of inventing meaning; people remain a product of their history.

Whether we like it or not, we cannot think or speak about ourselves or about others outside the conceptual parameters by which we are—involuntarily—bound.

Representations of identity (both individual and collective) that emerged in European history are without a doubt part of these groundbreaking ideas upheld by a modernity intent on uprooting certainties. This was the result of two convictions that even today appear irrefutable: one, the notion that individuals exist, act, and are perceived as indivisible, substantive, and self-governing; and, two, that they are by nature rational, autonomous, and free. In this sense, the modern perspective about the place of man in society was not arrived at by a transhistorical being that was free from innate qualities. Rather, it referred to a being that perceives itself as fundamentally and inherently free. The transition from a natural to an ideological conceptualisation of man[11] was a radical shift following which identity started going through the transcendental idea of liberty: one couldn't think well if one didn't think freely.

This was nothing short of a revolution in the history of ideas, maybe one of the most significant since the invention of gods.[12] Ideas and representations of human nature and society need constant redefinition through this basic and inalienable value that defines collective paradigms.[13] In this sense, neoliberalism's victory has been sweeping—even those that are in the opposite political camps seem to be inspired by the same universal moral origins. The demand for emancipation seems unassailable.

But this fixation with individual liberty has costly consequences for societies. If people are perceived as supposedly self-ruling, collectives are not. And if by virtue of being independent ethical units, free individuals make decisions and weigh their values against external prescriptions[14], then they must always be able to choose (or at least negotiate for themselves) the terms of their consent to social-isation. All modern ideas about personal and collective identities must appear, directly or indirectly, compatible with both the principal value of personal liberty *and* with those terms.

Cohesion doesn't appear out of thin air. In order to prevail historically, new collective identities must be forged through a series of arduous and systematic ideological interventions. The typically modern mechanisms of socialisation which inured individuals to new values and conceptual systems served precisely that purpose.[15] In order for people to share and promote their natural abilities within a finite social setting, they must know well the limits of their autonomous individuality, as well as the rules that govern their participation in a community. Before it can prevail, the idea of liberty must be established in the collective imaginary.

Autonomous individuals
and subservient communities

An important and new issue had surfaced: for the first time, modern liberalism was required to defuse and rationalise the tension between an autonomy naturally [16] inherent in people, and the rational prescriptions of a free and at the same time compulsory participation in subservient collectives. In this way, the question of combining personal liberty with legitimised social authority surfaced not only as a persistent philosophical, socio-political, and ideological challenge, but as a historical riddle. In order to achieve the harmonious cohabitation of the free *I* and the indispensable *we*, individualism has to appear compatible with social, national, and sovereign prescriptions. People need to participate in a collective that demarcates the limits of freedom, without this participation appearing to be compromising it. The logical dead end is obvious.

We shouldn't be surprised that neoliberalism oscillates awkwardly between two equally negative and inescapable theoretical constructs. Although on the one hand, biological, social, or political determinism appears logically incompatible with freedom [17], the vagueness of absolute free will appears, on the other, incommensurable with the idea of coexistence within a cohesive collective [18].

To deal with this antinomy, the modern world had to invent new intellectual tools and rationalising tricks. In contrast to premodernity, where authority was explicitly declared and imposed from the top down (and was therefore automatically reproducible), organised liberal societies needed to find ways to recognise and respect the free individuality of their members whilst making sure that, in reality, personal freedom never slipped into unruliness. Like culture produced within institutions that are by design restrictive, the culture of freedom is historically inseparable from the rationalisation and demarcation of historically and logically specific restrictions of free cohabitation. Following the death of God and the weakening of His will, free people must simultaneously be taught the abstract meaning *and* the specific limits of their freedom.[19]

This antinomy which runs in the veins of the neoliberal fantasy, about a community of freely disposed people, found expression in the design and safeguarding of the most important institutional, political, and ideological achievements of modernity. By legally consecrating personal liberties, the rule of law, and the internalisation of categorical imperatives, neoliberal societies acquired their distinct moral flesh and their institutional bones. And yet, despite their outreach, these constructs still didn't solve the contradiction. The theoretical and psychological incompatibility of personal freedom and the binding nature of laws and regulations remained conceptually irresolvable and historically unsettled. In this sense, to the degree that, as Jeremy Bentham admitted, every law is against freedom[20], the relationship between autonomy and social rule remains still irresolvably tense. This tension explains why the issues of conditionality and domestication of personal liberty have been from day one the primary subjects of liberal political philosophy.

Freedom cannot be exercised with moderation. Like desire, free will is "a cry for what one is, just as one is, at any given moment"[21], a cry that transcends logic, snubs causality, surpasses lucidity[22] and intentions[23]. The object of desire acquires meaning as simultaneous presence and absence, as allusion to an impossible completeness, as provocation and deprivation. It cannot but surrender to the great and unpredictable whirl of a mad *allegro maestoso e barbaro*, closing its ears to the whispering of a restraining *ma non troppo*. The trick that allowed Ulysses to enjoy the Sirens' song doesn't work as a universal rule. Maybe it's because "you never know what is enough, unless you know what is more than enough"[24], that personal freedom is expressed always as a discretion or ability not just of using but also of *abusing*[25] uncontrollable urges, unfulfillable desires, and undisclosed intentions.

Modern liberal societies never give up trying to square the moral circle. The attraction of free people to the rules and regulations of mandatory incorporation into wider institutionalised regulatory systems doesn't prevent them from wanting to test the limits of their relationship with others. But limiting people, with or without their consent, *must* remain a possibility. And, as Rousseau said, for a person to learn to exercise and manage their freedom whilst avoiding widespread anomie, there must be a contract that doesn't just coerce but also persuades and convinces. Of course, contracts neither can nor could lead to final solutions to the problems they create; they simply help put in motion conceptually vague, politically negotiable, and always ambiguous and fragile historical *compromises.*

The issue of securing social order and orderliness therefore continues to remain logically controversial and historically open. This might be the reason why the Swiss philosopher was himself convinced that what was needed was a *civil religion*[26] that would coat iron logic with a transcendental glaze. Since simple affirmations of social unity and law and order remain necessarily fragile and revocable, the need arises to devise an additional, illusory if need be, safety valve that guarantees their perpetuation and reproduction. The cohesion of a collective which itself is the result of a contract, is always under threat of potential resistance or retraction by the constitutively unpredictable counterparts.[27] What is it that makes an everlasting collective of people remain always a people? And how can we be sure that democratic minorities will not break away as ideological and political minorities—or, even, be reshaped into subversive factions? Both questions are unanswerable, at least so if considered within a pure neoliberal individualistic frame. Historical solutions to such riddles can only be achieved by making an ideological leap.

Nation as civil religion

Turning, then, a stable and firm union of people into an organised society requires that everyone comes to regard the latter as natural and obvious. This can only be achieved through a collectively shared imaginary about a historically formed and perpetually reaffirmed cultural distinctiveness. This exclusive, distinct, and identifiable national spirit (what Herder called *Volksgeist*) is something that all societies naturally have—and have to have. The appearance of choice, even if it retrospectively reveals itself to have been the *only* choice, must be maintained. In order for collectivity to persist in its perpetuation as an organised dominion, it must first be constructed self-reflexively, and then contextualised within time and history.[28]

This is why new identities depend on some (real or imaginary) homogeneous provenance.[29] It is indeed ironic that Rousseau's civil religion ended up disguised as the Herderian national spirit and refined through now-fetishised collective national substantiations. History, stubbornly resisting rationalisation, invented and imposed the best possible solution. Homogeneous provenance offered the ideological foundations necessary for the processing of a new national theology within which the material body of the contract-bound people was able to emerge as *corpus mysticum*. And, as it happened in premodern past, it appeared as *corpus fictum*, *corpus imaginatum*, and *corpus representatum*.[30]

In this sense, the birth of the homogeneous modern nation far exceeds the historical and factual material that its subsequent narrative unravelling produced.[31] The idea of *nation* as the provider of invaluable conceptual mediation between the notions of freedom and commitment, particular and general[32], and individual and collective, came to be a necessary addition to the historically precarious and inadequate idea of a contractually organised society of free individuals.[33] Although free people are responsible for choosing the terms of participation in their contractual polity, it is also beyond doubt that they remain culturally thrown into this non-negotiable natural nation and soaked in the national blood that runs through its veins.[34] To achieve this, nations must appear omnipresent, as having existed before and regardless of democratic or contractual consents and consciences. It follows that collectivity—by evoking so-called *natural* forms of individual and collective commitments that precede free choice and fall beyond the reach of any rationalising process[35]—emerged well before it revealed, named, and organised itself historically. The unifying potential of collectivity resists Forster's plea to be given the strength to betray his country (which he couldn't have chosen) rather than betraying his friends (which he freely chose), and this is apparent in the timelessness of the idea of a substantiated nation. It is not surprising that every time in modern history that secular regimes found themselves under threat, they did not employ some merely contractual, civic, or class-related rhetoric. Rather, they resorted to arousing the idea of a substantiated nation. Aware that imaginary truths are stronger, French people defended their Revolution with the motto *la patrie en danger* (the country in peril); and the Soviets brought up Alexander Nevsky and Ivan the Terrible in order to convince the new socialist people to defend their eternal Russian motherland from the Teutonic invaders. The survival and maturation of sovereignty, nation, the state, and national culture requires a unifying conceptual, symbolic, and prescriptive order.

All of this shows that, regardless of actual historical origins pertaining to the foundation of national communities, new collective identities must be standardised, idealised, and, most importantly, reproduced. It follows that the main concern of emergent nation-states has been inventing those relevant and necessary ideological mechanisms that would guarantee systemic creation and propagation.[36] In order to produce their unifying results, customs and traditions had to be invented, reconstituted, and systematised as parts of a coherent narrative that could promise perpetuation. Collective memory contributes massively to the formation of an existing identity, even if such memory neither discovers nor invents it[37].

In the case of new ideological mechanisms established by modern states, collective memory became, then, the object of conscious and systematic nurturing. This has been the most important historical function of education in modern times.[38] Official language, state religion, ethnic social mores and customs, grammatology, geography, and, most importantly, a history that attests to the historical transcendence of national continuity: these are more than just shards of cold, stale knowledge; they are the essential pre-contractual elements that provide an engaged calling which, in turn, guarantees socialisation.[39] This was the single most decisive contribution of national intelligentsias in the founding of the new social powers. As Karl Kraus said, "Origin is the goal"[40]. In order for imaginary identities and false consciousnesses to carry on well into the infinite and uncertain future, it must remain possible that they can be anchored to a conceptually definite and clear past which, to quote Borges, "occupies in our memories the place of another, a past of which we know nothing with certainty— not even that it is false"[41]. This in no way suggests that the past is less enchanting, less alive, or even less plausible; quite the opposite—truth is by no means the supreme cognitive value.[42]

National societies were thus hardened through historically novel forms of ideological violence. By teaching people (or simply coercing them into believing) that they are free creators of a contract-based collective and that they are obliged to identify with their substantiated public personality and engage in their 'natural' historical cultural group, newly instituted powers constructed zealous members of transhistorical and transcendental nations who were also free, yet law-abiding, citizens of a historical rule of law. The political demand to reproduce legitimate power was combined with the concurrent demand for imaginary uniformity and cohesion. Historicised cultural singularity, contractual founding, and collective identity were organised inside the frame of a common, centrally articulated, robust, multifaceted, and conceptually holistic rhetoric. For the first time in history, (national) lawful political power, (national) culture, (national) territory, and (national) sovereignty were constructed as parallel cognitive fields and were idealised as corresponding normative conquests.

The exclusive status
of national substantiations

This, however, is hardly good enough. The idea of national identity, at least in its standardised form, must also be capable of outweighing, superseding, substituting, and, if necessary, suppressing and stifling any potentially competing new identities, whether subversive or not. This explains why the substantiated idea of a nation cannot ever tolerate deviance from or opposition to its stereotypical and fetishised transhistorical orthodoxy[43]. It is in this context that the relations of national identity and any other kind of collective identification have been shaped. It should not surprise us that the modern nationalistic rhetoric appears a priori exclusive and holistic; all *other* imaginary identities must acknowledge its supremacy. Identities that are seen as consubstantial and convergent to the national identity (as in the case, wherever it applies, of state religions) are fortified and supported together with the dominant one (of the primary nation).[44] Those, on the other hand, that are perceived as threats face contempt, even eradication. Like all monotheisms, totalitarian and national monotheism does not accept other aspiring gods, be they 'known' or not.[45]

We should note that this demand for exclusivity is directly and strikingly inconsistent with what used to happen in premodern times: in most traditional societies, people could simultaneously belong to various different and symbolically fluctuating groups (formed on the basis of local, blood, racial, ancestral, religious, political, dynastic, or even personal co-dependency bonds).[46] Premodern holisms were not necessarily unifying and 'identificational'. Communities, societies, powers, and hierarchies were reproduced simply by being there. Collective identity was not a political concern, and powers were created and reproduced in spite of it.

By contrast, in modernity the a priori hegemony of a unique and at the same time exclusive national identity[47] was for the first time institutionalised as necessary, natural, and unquestionable. Even if man was free to choose what he identified with, the ideological and political tendency to have a righteously homogeneous national body was unassailable. What can be loosely called *national* became the object of an unprecedented socialisation process fixated on the idea of a nation—a socialisation that existed before and extended beyond free choice as such. Following Rousseau's, Herder's, and Fichte's prescriptions, incorporation into the rules of common cohabitation appeared as the ineluctable and self-evident objective of a wide, common, and internally cohesive mechanism of mass prose-lytisation to the symbolic demands of an all-encompassing national, civic, and ideological identity. And, in this sense, the distinctive rationale of national socialisation was the structuring of holistic and inclusive collective identities that could remain forever unchangeable and could ve-hemently resist slipping into uncertainty. National exclusivity, being the child of a fetishised past, reaching far into the endless hereafter—this was the major historical wager.

Minorities as a historical irony

But history again had the last laugh. Taking the con-stant reshuffling of power balances and the subse-quent changes in those powers' limits into account, the timelessness of national constructs conflicted constantly with the real and imaginary historical instability of unincorporated—often nameless—populations that inhabited the national territories. The political demand for imaginary uniformity of the power classes contradicted the natural geopolitical and 'geocultural' diversity and imper-manence of an ever-moving, complicated, chaotic, and unclassifiable reality. This rendered contractu-al societies contingent and provisional; even, one might argue, negotiable.[48] And it also gave rise to the notorious question of minorities.

We call *minorities* those groups of people that for a number of reasons (religious, linguistic, economic, geographic, racial, or simply reactionary) either resisted from the start the homogenising nationalism imposed on them, or were forced to submit to national polities that they perceived as oppressive, foreign, and unfamiliar. The discourse, determined to transubstantiate and subsume those refractory and disruptive groups into recognisable, conforming, and eligible minorities[49], was conceived as a response to the opposing holistic and exclusive nationalistic discourse. This, incidentally, accounts for the historical similarities between the discourses of nations and minorities. The fetishised national imaginary community and the equally fetishised minority imaginary community appear historically inseparable and logically co-dependent, and at the same time ideologically opposed.

Indeed, following the example of nations, minorities too banked on their distinct culture, narrated their exclusive (hi)story, and wove their collective memory with one end in mind: reproduction of their individual and substantiated essence. They only differ from actual nations in that they (still) lack their own land and their own organised sovereignty. This means that they are not in position to effect their *own* social contract inside their *own* social territory, and are therefore perpetually politically unfulfilled and ideologically blood-drenched. And it is for this reason that they tend to advance absurd and practically unattainable territorial demands.[50] It shouldn't surprise us that the openly voiced ambition of most minorities is to historically transform themselves into complete sovereign nations (like the 'others'), enabling the conversion of their blood-drenched minority essence into a tangible national spirit. Seen in this light, and considering the perpetually reshuffling geopolitical order, it becomes clear that the rhetoric employed by minorities does not at all constitute a historical anomaly; rather, it is the standard way of things. This is why it tends to be treated (and is often suppressed) as a highly dangerous political and normative irregularity. Curiously, it is nations themselves that nurture the preconditions for the historical appearance of the very minorities that they then proceed to discredit.

The rhetoric employed by minorities (and the discourse revolving around their unique identity) found itself from the start under severe pressure from logical scrutiny. Only those groups that managed to use to their advantage the key criterion of national uniformity were acknowledged. In order to gain the legal, political, cultural, and, most importantly, historical privileges (accorded always by common sentiment and the legal powers in which it is crystallised) that can guarantee their formal and symbolic recognition[51] (which, in turn, will 'upgrade' them to special and protected national or religious collective entities), minorities must exhaust their historical resources and prove themselves worthy of participating in power games. Being well aware that the unforgiving current of history is threatening them with gradual appropriation and extinction, they have only one option: to swim against it.

We must stress that successful admission was in no way achieved because minorities exercised some universally accepted 'right to self-determination' or, even less so, right to difference. Contrary to common perceptions, the rights and privileges enjoyed by minority groups were never granted from above, or conferred in line with moral truisms and universal principles. They were always earned through long and in most cases strenuous political and ideological struggles. It is only thanks to the fortuitous grasping of historical opportunities that some minorities were able to establish their presence in the shifting tables of conflicting powers and interests. Marching under the Caudine yoke of merciless history, very few groups actually managed to earn the privilege of dictating the terms of their reproduction and socialisation in defiance of the incontestable uniformity of the national (civic) societies that accommodated them.[52] Like Marx said about the Jews: they survived *because* of history, not against it—and history's judgement is, by definition, prejudiced.

Summing-up: until recently, systems of collective cultural reference were instituted and substantiated on the basis of cultural distinction from others. Because of this, rationalistic modern government determines its exclusive subjects, demarcates its exclusive jurisdiction, and institutes its exclusive symbolic order. The actual demarcation of space[53] and control of national territory is augmented by the regulatory enclosures of political sovereignty, the narrative enclosures of substantiated historical continuity, the ideological enclosures of cultural standards, and finally the imaginary enclosures of collective imaginaries. The shape of modern ideological hegemony uncannily resembles a much wider (if compared to the premodern past) substantiation of interconnected holistic exclusivities. *Cuius regio, eius religio* gave its place to *cuius regio, eius populatio, territorium, lex, lingua, historia* and *memoria*. Or, to use more ominous terms: *ein Volk, ein Staat, eine Kultur, eine Geschichte*; and when the need arises, *ein Lebensraum* and perhaps *ein Führer*.

4

GLOBALISATION
Upending Realities, Erasing Meanings

The world is changing rapidly. Globalisation is not just reshaping the structure of economies and the organisation of labour and production—it is also changing the dominant conceptual schemes, the meaning of, ideas behind, and exercise and rationalisation of power. In recent years, traditional taxonomies, certitudes, and tools used for understanding selfhood, otherness, and the social collective have evaporated. In this new landscape, representations of identities—personal and collective—no longer conform to their conceptual origins. When societies cease to be perceived as a shared, self-sufficient, and fetishised *Volksgeist*, the terms of ideological identification and incorporation into the social collective must be revised. In order to deal with the spectre of structural disjointedness, institutional powers are forced to invent new justifications and legitimations. Lurking entropic tendencies are, thus, no longer contained through the conventional use of brute direct ideological violence. Nor is the issue of perpetuating social cohesion addressed by ritually expelling centrifugal tendencies. Nowadays, social and ideological divergences are not suppressed; on the contrary, they are rationalised, idealised even. The end of grand narratives[1] that heralded the arrival of the postmodern world seems to go hand in hand with the end of grand exclusions.

Space and time

There's been a momentous shift in perceptions of a unified society as that combination of confined territory, independent lawful civic order, and self-perpetuating symbolic unity. Changes on this front are immediately obvious. The cross-fertilisation of revolutionary scientific and technological breakthroughs, the realisation of a globalised market, the spectacular speeding up of communications and transportation, and the mobility of decision makers themselves have all contributed in weakening the distinction between in and out—not only in the financial and political spheres but, most crucially, in the symbolic reach of these terms themselves and in the semantics that guaranteed this very distinction. The birth of these new coordinates means that space can no longer be organised in concentric circles that share the same stable symbolic and functional middle points.[2] The distance that separated points of solid spatio-temporal orderings has lost its meaning; the dividing lines have lost their reach. Depending on the moment and point of view, everything can be near or far, everything can simultaneously assume interior, exterior, or consecutive positions along a Möbius strip that lacks a discernible up/down, forward/backward, or in/out.[3] When everything is moving, motion is not determined by space; it *determines* it.[4]

This affects the relation of people to space. National territories that were heretofore enclosed and unquestionably solid are now expected to accommodate moving denizens and occasional visitors who, even when physically *somewhere*, they are potentially *anywhere*, and thus appear to be *nowhere*. In the context of this global *Völkerwanderung*, which could be the largest the world has even seen, indigenous residents are asked to coexist, mingle, associate with, and compete against all sorts of visible and invisible neighbours, settlers, foreigners, travellers, even vagrants and homeless drifters 'without qualities'. The unrestrained opening up of space means that the imaginarily sealed, conceptually solid, and symbolically self-sufficient national territories survive only as wistful memories of an age long gone. The old explicit *limits* have been replaced by ambiguous and uncertain *thresholds*, where everything is *in between*.[5] Suddenly, taxonomic uncertainty seems to be everywhere.[6]

What's more, together with the connotations of space, the crucial psychological significance of shared social space has also changed. When ideas about the social stability of a historically integrated whole and its collective continuity are torn down, when the fetishised historical *Volksgeist* is weakened, and when the ability to reduce events to a single origin and a binding national destiny are lost, existential angst and uncertainty soar. The map of human life, deprived of its landmarks, no longer obeys reassuringly prearranged regulations.[7] Fixed points of reference are deregulated, de-emphasised, moved to unknown locations. In this way, symbolic absences and gaping voids obscure all traditional, familiar, and stable presences.[8] What provided disoriented travellers with a refuge has disappeared. It shouldn't surprise us that when the coordinates of social coexistence within a shared space, time, and semantic matrix cease to adhere to standard prescriptions, people start feeling increasingly vulnerable. Disorientation brings the weakening of identifications, of symbolic bastions, and of comforting reflexes.

Mobility of the means of production

Space and time's symbolic collapse affect capitalist market relations. The most apparent trait of globalisation is unfettered mobility; mobility of means of production, of capital, of labour, and most conspicuously, mobility of private information, expertise, and intellectual property. This has had catalytic effects. Contrary to what was still the case as recently as thirty years ago, the question of isolating, delineating and protecting a national financial territory[9], an industrial and agricultural production, a national currency, and also labour relations, labour peace, social issues, and a bourgeoisie, appears to be a meaningless souvenir.

In this volatile, opportunistic, and totally erratic relationship between people and their spatio-temporal realities, the indefatigably mobile labour force that desperately looks for ways and places of provisional sustenance and the instantaneously movable capital (which more often than not aims for short-term financial gains) both behave like nomads who wander and survive in an open and unrestricted world.[10] For the first time in history, the world game is perambulatory, vagrant, deceptive[11], and global. All places appear operationally equivalent.

Production relations everywhere are saturated with the same instrumental opportunism: on the one hand, masses of wretched people (migrants or not) roam the world, driven by a despair that makes them take any risk in order to temporarily secure survival. And, on the other, moseying capitalists pursue profit maximisation by deciding at any given moment on what, where, under what terms, for how long, and how much they will invest. All spaces of production end up functioning identically; multiplicity is eliminated; all places have essentially become *one*.

And that's not all. The unyielding logic of free-market capitalism has caused remarkable transformations on the market's very function. Since a substantial share of transactions is carried out opportunistically and ad hoc, the significance of extra-market social ties is trivialised. Increasingly more exchanges are nowadays negotiated as single-shot games where the expectations of the participants are exhausted in one-off deals; neither party makes any assumptions for future dealings. Conversely, the contraction of the transactional space means that the significance of mutuality and trust is weakened.[12] Paradoxically, then, when relations become structurally opportunistic, cold-blooded capitalist utopia reaches its culmination.[13] By weakening all informal mechanisms of control over social reciprocity, the blind, unsparing, and self-regulating market seems to sew up all social relations.[14] This has profound repercussions in transactional ethics and conventions. The constant exchange of people and institutions that engage in negotiations of material goods, services, and labour not only eliminates the need for the account and client books but, most importantly, it renders credibility and reputation in the marketplace obsolete.[15] Operating anonymously, the free market seems to be reaching a quintessential individualistic perfection it could until recently only dream of.

As a result, common forms of what was considered *rational* financial behaviour tend to be systematised in the most perfect, pure, and extreme class form. In future, opportunistic investors will only be interested in maximising their immediate returns, whereas the sole concern of those who find themselves intermittently employed will be to survive another day. The strategic pursuits of both opposed social classes are determined by an equally short-sighted opportunism. Even if production is tied to a specific place and time, the financial times and places are organised in ways that only exceptionally factor in the distant future. It is, therefore, normal that the regulatory controls of transactional practices are focused only on formal flawlessness.

The relationship of financial and political powers has similarly changed. The global mobility of transnational funds and capitals (assisted by the uncontrollable proliferation of obscure offshore havens) led to further organisational and regulatory unfettering and release from state control. Like Attila, financiers can now move in a borderless wilderness where they ride in, profiteer, launder, extort and appropriate[16], destroy, cash out, and then (like Paul Klee's *Angelus Novus* in the reading rendered by Walter Benjamin[17]) set off, turning a blind eye to the piling hecatomb they leave behind. Spectacularly juxtaposed to the organically assimilated capitalists of the past (who organised their enterprise and extracted the majority of their profit within the confines of the societies in which they operated and with which they identified), they have no use for long-lasting (real or symbolic) ties with their nation-states. Following the example set by the shipping industry (or, even, of the pirates that wandered *sans dieu ni maître*), they are pleased just sailing the open and uncontrolled seas of moving circumstances and profit opportunities. The unprotected and powerless political powers have fewer options than ever. This is maybe why, turning necessity into open-handedness, they so frequently yield—willingly or not—to the inexorable callings of the corsairs.

The relation between political and financial powers

In this same context, we should look at the deterioration of the conceptual preconditions necessary for the enforcement of organised political power. Although they often go unmentioned, changes on this front are equally historic. Despite the fact that liberal-democratic powers appeared already institutionally restricted and insufficient (in the sense that their possibilities were limited by inalienable individual rights[18] and by the terms of augmenting a legitimate constitutional sovereignty), the potential reach of modern liberal states is subject to informal and implicit, but much more substantial and unpredictable, external limitations. Even in the context of their official duties, states appear to increasingly abstain from intervening on issues pertaining to the preservation of social ties and the promotion of public welfare and prosperity. As a result, the terms used for describing and understanding the relations of political and financial powers have been revised. The relative autonomy that the capitalist state enjoyed against financial powers seems to change, not only as far as structural prescriptions are concerned, but also in terms of the scale to which this autonomy is exercised and organised, the historical operations that activate it, and the purposes that it serves.[19]

Even more so considering that, contrary to what happened historically, the new limitations and constraints are not so much institutional, legal, or constitutional as they are political and ideological—one could even consider them *irrational*. These constraints are connected to the widespread sway of two distinct but interconnected dogmas. On the one hand, the philosophical dogma that social progress is, if not entirely tantamount, then at least directly related to economic growth[20]; and, on the other, the utilitarian dogma that this growth can only be achieved by setting transactional practices and the market as a whole free. Operating in these conditions, political power is unable, unwilling, or simply afraid to intervene in socio-economic events in any way other than to support the developmental agenda of further market liberation.

The long-term combined effects of these two dogmas have been literally world-changing.[21] Since the 1950s[22] (and possibly as a response to the theoretical proclamations and rationalisations of socialist economies[23]), when economic growth[24] was posited at the centre of the liberal political discourse[25], the hitherto open and debatable historical and political normativity has become completely and universally subjugated to a rigid and ideologically airtight development mantra that doesn't take *no* for an answer. With a stroke of the pen, age-old debates revolving around political priorities suddenly disappeared. Irrespective of consequences, *all* political decisions were made to comply with a categorical need for growth. It seems inevitable then, that in the context of a preordained course even the last remnants of the traditional regulatory framework of social cohesion and solidarity were discarded as an irrelevant, historically *passé*, useless, and contemptible weight.[26] Development *as such* seems to trump everything else. The autonomous moral foundation of politics as an open, constantly reflective, never-ending critical debate around collective normativity belongs to the past. The heralded end of history logically precludes political ideology and morality.

As such, the manifest triumph of economic deregulation is only the other side of the gradual effectuation of political deregulation and the extra-political (over-)regulation of the understanding of public good. If we continue to define politics as that collectively organised social subsystem whose mission is the promotion of a universally endorsed notion of 'the good', then we must really wonder whether politics as we knew it still exists. From the moment that actual political objectives are negotiated and settled outside the scope and without the participation of organised political powers[27] (meaning, decided by groups that control the movement of capital, knowledge, technology, and information), then what we today persist to call *political* has ceased being precisely that. The managerial and developmentally oriented agenda, committed as it is to utilitarian maximisation, is finally free to circumvent its eternal immersion into indecision and unresponsiveness.[28] Politics, no longer fit to formulate and enforce action that originates in an actively self-instituted will, seems to have lost its inherent boldness, its very definition as that space where dominant collective action is embodied, its *raison d'être*. The persistent decline of its credibility should therefore not surprise us. Political vision, moving within the confines of its structural subservience, seems to have surrendered its crucial duty to unqualified hands: to the unaccountable, unaffected, invisible, and untrustworthy hands of private interests. Everything is happening as if the liberal national, civic, and political theology has finally capitulated to a universal techno-economic theology.[29] Being completely de-politicised and de-ideologicised, the prophets are content to obey the gods of privatised financial rationalism.

On sovereignty and 'post-sovereignty'

All the above is ultimately related to the (historical, legal, ideological) issue of weakening, relativising, and historicising the idea of national sovereignty— an idea that since the Treaty of Westphalia (1648) has been considered indispensable to the notion of a modern European state.[30] Unsurprisingly, the concrete concept of sovereignty has been replaced by the vague notion of post-sovereignty.[31] In today's world, in fact, the social preconditions necessary to satisfy Carl Schmitt's definition of the sovereign as the one who decides on the exception have shifted.[32] The debasement of political power continues to be explained, vindicated, and rationalised as the result of invariably extrinsic and semi-permanent *states of emergency*[33] that can only be addressed using off-the-peg policies. This political voicelessness is directly linked to a spectacularly shrunk range of available choices. (It was precisely this development that the Thatcherite *There Is No Alternative* foretold.) Political powers constantly invoke a real or imagined emergency so that they can act in the service of developmental priorities; everything else can wait. Free from moral, aesthetic, or political uncertainty, Caliban can now see his reflection in the mirror without being daunted by the disgusting sight. Politics, trapped in the unsavoury role of a conscientious yet obedient and taciturn middleman between a wretched reality and its efficient management, can hide behind its moral colour-blindness.

The now permanent invocation of an externally imposed demand has institutionalised a new administrative procedure of reproducing subservient political powers that *welcome* their subservience.[34] These rationalised political systems are limited to administering and managing unpredictable external demands, troubles, and crises with the use of predefined prioritisation criteria and out-of-the-box solutions. The universal degradation of political vocabulary is, therefore, normal (words are anyway never entirely innocent). Indicatively, the etymological root of the generic term *administration* betrays its original meaning: being of service to someone. A *minister* is one who acts on the orders of others, and in medicine, *to administer* is *to provide. Administration*, then, describes a type of government that does not *govern*, but *facilitates*. This in itself signals a change in the ways of perceiving, understanding, and doing politics. Until recently, the conflict between *order* and *administration* could be implemented within a semantic matrix[35] in which the former enjoyed precedence. The recasting of growth-oriented market economy into an unassailable extra-political influencer, however, saw the age-old idiosyncrasy of politics proper shifting decisively. Like *progress*, the ambiguous notions of *common good* and *common sense* are no longer the objects of genuine contemplation, but of decision-making. This, it seems, was the objective.

We are witnessing a radical uprooting of the past, and the beginnings of a new historical cycle. If, as Michel Foucault pointed out, modernity is characterised by the fact that power relations hitherto manifested primarily in war have moved to the political sphere[36], then current developments are even more historic. The few remaining emasculated and dilapidated orders of political power are replaced by still-undefinable orders of unregulated power networks that are legitimised by a 'common-sensical' order of things. This means that a rationalistic type of relationship between politics and economy has been substantiated as the only possible one.[37] The bourgeoisie can finally see its repressed fantasy of a blind political power that is automatically and efficiently exercised[38] (a government, in other words, that has no use for a mediating and potentially contingent political subsystem which can always abuse its conferred power) come to life.

Discrediting publics

Besides practical considerations as such, the weakening of national jurisdictions and powers, the enfeeblement of society's self-instituting potential[39], the transposition of governing centres to obscure, unregulated, extra-territorial, and extra-political 'out theres', and the disappearance of public responsibility are all reflected in the systematic downgrading of public space and of the symbolic potency of politics proper. Additionally, the increasing osmosis of public and private spheres, the discrediting of the notion of welfare, and the overall stigmatisation of the objective ability (and also authority) of states to negotiate and resolve moral issues and settle major social problems compromise the importance of the traditionally central institutional and ideological place that public space had within the wider system of social symbolisms. The operations of the state appear like necessary evils that must be minimised.

The emancipation of states from their historically established moral origins appears, then, inescapable, ordinary, expected. It is not surprising to observe that the old ideas of social justice, lenience, and solidarity don't seem to be the obvious and unswerving moral and political priorities they once were. And, even if these fundamental moral origins cannot be entirely eradicated from the collective imaginary, they are nonetheless applied only *in extremis*, in the form of a cursory duty towards those *completely* deprived of any chance of sustenance (and only in particular—read: favourable—circumstances).[40] This is indeed a historic ideological transformation. For the first time in a century, social issues appear marred by the merciless forces of development. State minimalism, unfettering of public space from its exclusive ideological and moral obligations, and disintegration of the educational and welfare public monopolies are all manifestations of what appears to be an unchallengeable socio-political dogma.

Unsurprisingly, the internal functions of the organised state are also challenged. Henceforth, all public institutions are to be seen as either intrinsically or potentially irrational, burdensome, unproductive, and *bureaucratic*[41]. In the name of progress, efficiency, and common practical sense, the anorexic state can and *should* limit its interventions as much as possible; in other words, it should only do what cannot be done by (meaning it is financially adverse to) free market enterprise. The predominance of the development rhetoric leaves no room for other ways of measuring the importance of institutions outside that of their estimated contribution to development. As the historical epitome of a rational, solidary, lenient, and human system of market relations that enjoys the legitimacy that its moral standards provide, the social state is dying.

Ideological individuation and introversion

Directly related to the questions raised at the beginning of this chapter, the final set of observations focuses on the socio-psychological developments that affect the way individuals understand their place in the world and their relation to society. If, as Freud claimed, civilisation manifests itself as a historical trade-off between freedom and security, it seems apparent that today the latter has retreated in favour of the former.[42] In this field, the most important event is the completion of ideological individuation. In the systematically meta-solidary and (in-name-only) anti-holistic societies that are emerging, individuals are not socialised as members of a wider and fixed organic whole within which they are expected to find a place (social class, ideology, or profession) that suits them. Instead, they are produced as free, naked, and self-governing competitive individuals of whom it is expected that they will realise their dreams and define themselves by substantiating their personalised productive usefulness, adaptability, employability—and, in this way, acquire their worth.

This has a number of consequences: from the moment that organised societies tend to dispose of their traditionally pastoral[43], symbolic, and moral roles, and free people can build their self-esteem using only their own resources, their relation to the whole abstractly, and to others specifically, will be radically transformed. On the one hand, people no longer need to be incorporated in a specific and homogeneous national community with the stringent and exclusive terms that applied in the past. On the other, they are urged to strive for the betterment of *only their own* life, *alone*. As free and responsible producers, planners, negotiators, and beneficiaries of their resources and skills, they are expected to minimise the presumably irrational pursuits and strategic actions that they might attempt together with others.[44] We are witnessing the slow but steady discrediting of all collectivities.[45]

Summing up: The normative terms of social relations are in the process of a decisive shift. Alongside that shift, the organised state is reordering its duties and responsibilities. The new calculative, responsible, and instrumentally efficient state cannot and *will not* be bothered with social justice and solidarity. It will wash its hands of anything that falls beyond those interventions, keeping in line with the rules that secure its place as an indifferent, impartial, and development-centred referee. By promising 'equal opportunities'[46] amongst coequal and self-differentiating free individuals, ensuring a 'fair' competition between individualised workers, and elevating law and order to a pivotal duty[47], the new political liberalism achieves all its goals. On one condition: that it keeps its duties to a minimum.

5

PERSONAL DESTINY

There is nothing new under the sun. Despite their flashy appearance, the ideological transformations of liberalism can be found in the emancipatory spirit of the Enlightenment. Like then, today's right to difference, the demand for cultural self-determination, and the ongoing campaign to expand liberties and the field of individuation are all emancipatory undertakings whose ultimate goal is to unchain individuals from the residues of illiberality that still appear to be stifling their autonomy. The rationale behind these ideological ventures appears entirely consistent with liberalism's original values. And if we endorse the hypothesis that the process of emancipation from real or imaginary ties is both constant and endless, then we must accept that it will stay forever unfinished.

The emergence of culture as a field for exercising individual rights and liberties has, however, consequences, of which the very choice of the word *culture* is telling. Indeed, culture has to be perceived as a generic category that, at least in theory, contains the totality of social practices. Inasmuch as there is nothing that takes place outside society (and therefore outside culture), furthering the demand for cultural emancipation effectively stretches the definition of the very word infinitely. Freedom from culture means unlimited freedom, and that means the ultimate victory of liberal ideals. The ratification of total cultural autonomy would mean that the Enlightenment is finally approaching its consummation.

But this kind of freedom surplus is simply impossible. Every society has to set limits. To the degree that the promise of cultural self-determination circumvents social regulations, it remains captive of an empty rhetoric and therefore doesn't seem to add much to the traditional libertarian ammunition. Like a *carte blanche*, it allows current circumstances to define its subject matter, and laws to determine its limits. Nothing new, then, on this front: already under the rule of old-style liberal dispensations, individuals were allowed to freely choose their beliefs, cultural codes, and attitudes, to conscientiously diverge from or openly oppose established cultural orthodoxies, and to individually or collectively promote whichever interests and concerns they wanted to, so long as they remained within the boundaries of the law. Already then— before it extended into culture—individual liberty was sanctioned in all its conceptual glory; any limitations were not conceptual *per se*, but historical, and therefore legal.

The fact that all of a sudden traditional liberalism appears unfulfilled and unfinished cannot be blamed on the functional inadequacy of the idea of liberty itself. Emancipatory deficiencies cannot be explained away as either conceptual or normative; they are always and by definition *historical*. Weighing its specific needs and priorities, every age advances and defends certain interpretations of the idea of liberty (and, by the same token, of the idea of constraint) over others. It also produces its own notions of autonomy and dependence, and outlines its own distinct emancipatory prescriptions. Meaning is always found between the lines. And this is why changes in the way those archetypal normative constructs are appropriated tend to reveal deeper, and often unseen, ideological shifts. The change of meaning that the idea of liberty has been invested with reflects historical transformations on the distorted mirror of liberal societies.

This is exactly where the historical essence of the current ideological departure begins to show its face: incorporated into the traditional liberal rationale, it perfects man's emancipatory ambition. After being freed from the (arbitrary) interventions of traditional powers, the new right to difference promises release from the—equally arbitrary and even oppressive—implicit ideological and symbolic ties that subject people to the reign of social customs and conventions.[1] The overspill of personal liberty into the realm that has been named *culture*—or *civilisation*[2]—serves this very purpose. Being patently indefinable and indeterminable, this space incorporates *all* the uninstitutionalised and opaque fields of thought and action that until now enjoyed the inexplicability that their obviousness afforded them. And, in this sense, culture includes much more than customary rational choices. In addition to the prerogative of the economic man to rationalistically strive for prosperity, cultural freedom opens up the possibility (and obligation) for the irrational and meta-rational person to find inner 'balance' and normative self-realisation.

Besides choosing their consciousness, thoughts, and actions, these 'culturally free' individuals must also invent and enforce the—often subconscious— terms of their social incorporation and ideological allegiances, their worldview, and their *à la carte* socialisation free from the traditional prescriptions of the society they find themselves in. Although obviously bound by laws, they are tasked with the non-negotiable duty to choose and organise their own self-differentiating conceptual orders, their personal cultural codes, their everyday social practices, and their habits. This is why the sphere of culture has been designated as the field of wider, open, and idiosyncratically delineated, privately sanctioned, and freely chosen creation, self-realisation, and pleasure.[3] It is now becoming widely accepted that, in order to establish an identity, individuals must be empowered with the freedom to construct, deconstruct, and freely choose their own personal culture. Which is, to say the least, an oxymoron.

Cultural difference as strategic choice

This is where postmodern rationalisations begin to show their structurally contradictory—utopian, even—character. A culture that hands the task of deciding and shaping the totality of normative and cultural aspects over to individuals, is a culture that has a priori forfeited the possibility of internal consistency and substantiation. Such a *culture of all possible cultures* is, simply, a *contradictio ad rem*.[4] If the right to difference implies unfettered ability to move freely along the entire range of possible behaviours and willy-nilly picking the terms of personal allegiances to or divergences from dominant worldviews, attitudes, and normative models[5], then this is tantamount to expecting that people would exist, think, and act as if independent of symbolic or contractual commitments—namely, outside society as such. Freely cultivating and impartially prioritising their beliefs, desires, and preferences, they would appear able to pick their own version of entrapment in a perfect ideological and normative solipsism. And, as unrestricted inventors of themselves, of their culture, of their principles and their mystifications, they would find themselves against a society that is also outside *them*.

This reverses the conceptual relation between individual difference and its socio-historical meaning. As Deleuze notes, "diversity is given, but difference is that by which the given is given", namely, the conceptual matrix in which diversity acquires meaning and value. Therefore, "difference is not phenomenon but the noumenon closest to the phenomenon"[6]. In this sense, the social weight and ethical meaning of difference can under no circumstances exist by itself as some transhistorical universalium—it can *only* occur as a result of, and in connection with, the definition that each society gives to the notion of *alterity*, meaning the degree of diversification of thought and action in relation to a state of affairs. In this sense, the meaning and limits of consensus and cultural tolerance can in no way remain stable and firm. In every society, and depending on prevailing conditions, the claim and realisation of individualised alterity can be treated as a simple and casual individual particularity, be registered as violation or as stigma[7], or—in the opposite direction—be warranted as fundamental and inalienable expression of the autonomous and untameable human nature. But it is the elevation of the right to difference into an *official ideology* that carries great historical importance.

From there on, individuals will not just be intrinsically distinct entities who think and act differently; they will additionally be obliged to live and make a living, responsible for the constant unravelling and exploiting of their own *constitutional* alterity. Constantly mutating, they will not be recognised as *naturally* different on account of the patent diversity of human acts and choices; they will instead be forced to identify with the *intentional* diversification of their individual plans and needs. From a practical perspective, sanctioning the right to difference appears concomitant with the widening of cultural horizons and self-knowledge. Alterity and difference are thenceforth signalled not as simple existential conventions of human life; they are elevated to rights that satisfy the needs and the vital interests of each person separately. And, in this sense, they are necessary strategic parameters of ratiocinative survival.

Laws, values, customs

The recognition of difference as a fundamental value gives it a new positive social meaning, and this raises another issue: from the moment that the right to self-differentiation is used as a protective shield against the widespread oppressive homogenising force of institutions and dominant norms and ideas, the impact and binding potential of all social regulations wanes. The result is that a new kind of tension between individual freedom and the need for social cohesion will emerge. Indeed, having been ousted from the secularised and fragmented national rule of law, the logical incompatibility between freedom and control which seemed to have somewhat subsided thanks to the liberal civic rationalisation is appearing again through the cracks of this decrepit construct—and this time it seems unstoppable. The ways of internalising the limits and limitations of liberty will have to be postulated anew. The normative foundations of the radically liberal society can no longer be licensed based on the obvious historical compromises of the contractual creature.

And this is not all. The relation between laws and customs—both being self-sufficient and interconnected sources of a common and solid regulatory order—can also no longer be what it used to. If the decree "I is a habit"[8] is true, this habit loses the endorsement of widely perceptible and reproducible unvarying social specifications. Until recently, laws and customs coexisted and cooperated within a consistent normative system.[9] From here on, the urgency of uninstituted and unlegislated cultural practices will not only be weakened, but deeply denigrated. The uninstituted cultural reflexes that served as commonly accepted webs of social conventionalities will lose their adhesiveness. In this regard, the quest for alterity functions as an antechamber to social and normative deviance from all possible orthodoxies: past, present, and future. The ideological structure and cohesion of society finds itself under tremendous strain.

Charles Taylor distinguishes between two forms of political liberalism.[10] On one side, a form of socio-political power whose main purpose is the protection of human rights of the citizens residing within a lawful order which must remain culturally impartial, neutral, and unprejudiced; and, on the other, a civic formation that is primarily focused on pursuing the reproduction of a complex social reality through the perpetuation of specific national, civic, cultural, and normative (and therefore to a degree, substantiated by tradition) standards.[11] It is in this conceptual framework that we can place the current quarrel between, on the one hand, unrepentant partisans who defend the undisguisedly strict and egalitarian republican politics and cultural neutrality and, on the other, zealots of a multicultural tolerance that can lead occasionally to incidents of reparatory favouritism.[12]

It is, of course, obvious that these two versions of liberalism have never existed in their pure form.

In fact, they can hardly be distinguished with any precision. But this is precisely what makes them historically and logically compatible. As we saw, already from its onset, political liberalism attempted a historical fusion of pure contractual forms and ethnocentric cultural substantiations. But for more than two centuries these issues could be eschewed. More than anything, the claim itself that this problem can today pose as a direct and urgent political challenge underscores the fact that when holistic cultural rationalisations subside, the civic discourse appears again incapable of resolving its internal inconsistencies. This is the setting of the endemic normative uneasiness of our times: when traditional contractual rationalisations subside, the question of the relation between individual and collective is again on the table. Back to square one.

Permission and prohibition

Naturally, under both (logically and historically extreme) versions, the insurmountable logical dead ends of the liberal rationalisation remain *de facto* irresolvable. Regardless of which solution we pick, the right to difference could never be unconditionally recognised. If a culture that included *all* possible forms of social practices became the object of free choice, the idea itself of a constituted cultural whole would become meaningless. Even if we momentarily ignored technicalities about the specific range of criteria, limits, and normative foundations of a volatile cultural tolerance, the issue itself of society's normative cohesion remains ineluctable: we simply cannot imagine a society that lacks an equally distributed system of ideological, symbolic, and normative principles. Even if each society institutes its own particular historical solutions, *some* solutions must be invented and enforced.

Even more so, considering that it's practically impossible to invent airtight transhistorical and logical principles that could help distinguish unrestricted individual action from action that complies with a minimum of shared cultural codes and norms (taboos). The interaction between what is and isn't allowed cannot be ignored.[13] To avoid widespread deregulation and general anomie, every organised society is obliged to breed some particular cultural codes, some common normative order, and some ways of deciding what is permitted and what is prohibited—and therefore what is normal and what is pathological.[14] No consolidated system of social relations could ever be founded on the *anything goes* principle. Something like that would require a degree of constitutional self-fragmentation that exceeds even Borges's imagination. No matter how extremely open it appears, multiculturalism could never be conceived of, or operate as, panculturalism.

In this sense, unconditional cultural tolerance and, even more so, the a priori recognition and protection of *all* eccentric cultural formations[15] would mean an absurd society that renounces its own right to control and suppress what it considers harmful and disruptive.[16] The delineation of what is permitted and tolerated, followed by the introduction of mechanisms for controlling unacceptable deviances—either as results of a conscious normative choice or as outcomes of unconscious social reflexes—are simply unavoidable historico-political conventions. All in all, the right to cultural self-determination is nothing more than a hollow invention with very limited historical sway that has managed to gain notoriety by systematically refusing to acknowledge that this right is by definition selective, and therefore controlled. Here we can begin to notice the power of pure ideology: the discourse on freedom, even when reality contradicts it, seems invincible.

And, despite the inherent inability to determine the content and set the limits of what is culturally permitted using strict criteria, the proclamation of the individual's right to difference has grave consequences. The political burden of proof regarding compatibility of those free (deviant or not) individual cultural choices with the mainstream is reversed. Instead of being obvious that citizens must on all occasions be socialised in line with customs and internalised regulations that comply with whatever are the dominant social values[17], people nowadays appear free from the outset to shape their cultural identity—in other words, to choose the terms of their personal (and of their family's[18]) socialisation—however they want[19]. It is not the necessity of regulations itself that is being questioned; it is the ways of *substantiating* this necessity. In this regard, the historical significance of current developments lies in that, in the context of the current legal order, and with the exception of *specific* choices that have been explicitly ruled out as being against the public order, each person has the right to choose *their* culture. Restrictive cultural rules are nowadays conceived of and enforced only retrospectively.

In this way, cultural compulsion and cultural and symbolic violence are not forgiven except sporadically, and only when they trigger important, essential, and inviolable principles of social cohabitation. In reality, however, this reversal remains rhetorical. It's impossible to have a priori historical, logical, or normative limits in the legal enforcement of a minimum of cultural orthodoxy. When they are confronted with (actual or perceived) threats of unacceptable regulatory, cultural, or political instability and anomie, governments always reserve the political prerogative to outlaw, restrict, or suppress cultural deviance. The recent prohibition of the chador in Belgium and France, for example[20], is undeniable proof that such states of cultural emergency can arise, be legitimised, and be sanctioned at any time and with any pretext. Even within such extremely tolerant and multicultural societies, as soon as the official powers feel that they must guard themselves against ideological and normative underminers, the historical potency of the dominant law wins out.[21]

Despite these restrictions, we are floating in the wake of a decisive transformation. It is telling that in most liberal democratic countries, centrally planned cultural interventions are becoming increasingly discreet, whilst cultural tolerance, neutrality, and even indifference[22] are becoming more common and more extensive. As we have witnessed, this development seems to go hand in hand with the universal prevalence of a wildly deregulatory neoliberalism. In this sense, the instituted and internalised *interventional minimalism* is not expressed only in the financial, productive, welfare, administrative, and—in the narrow sense—political field. The *laisser faire, laisser passer* dogma is also reflected on the level of normative standards, dominant ideologies, and the representations of the meaning of culture.

This is exactly where the radical break happened. To the extent that relations between these two fundamental and ruthlessly competitive elements of modern society—namely, the inviolable private space of individual liberty and the public space of compulsion and collective dominance—continue to be defined supplementally, the promise of expansion of the former can only happen at the expense of the interventional regulatory leverage of the latter.[23] In other words, regardless of explicitly redefining the duties and functions of the state, reinforcing an individualistic cultural model is increasingly contrasted with (a) the notion of a self-sufficient society, (b) the notion of a cohesive and committing culture, and (c) the notions of collective interest and general will. In our day, anything that has a bearing on the common political and cultural compulsion that accompanies public space seems to be in disarray. And when mechanisms of oppression are focused primarily on public order and security, the panoptic social control can successfully hide behind the idealisation of cultural impunity.

The Promise of
GUARANTEED EMPLOYMENT
Becomes the Nightmare of
LIFELONG LEARNING

Under pressure to negotiate the terms of their survival, people are now personally responsible for their uncertain fate. Having accepted the fact that others and society as a whole will not come to the rescue, they are left to strive for a (real or imaginary) place within this stratified system. Everything is unpredictable and uncertain: like both Sisyphus and Tantalus, they are forced to participate in a production process that can at any moment discard them as useless and redundant; to willingly consume the tokens of a symbolic prosperity that will eventually reveal itself to have been just a mirage; to oscillate between distractions that will only aggravate feelings of emptiness; and to maximise and exploit their skills while they still can. By developing strategies and preparing for a future that will more often than not lead to loss and denial, people have become responsible and accountable not only for their survival and their way of life, but also for the terms of their impending collapse and self-alienation. It is against this backdrop that we must analyse the social effects of the so-called *knowledge society*.

The age-old entitlement to *guaranteed employment*[1] is disappearing in favour of the topsy-turvy demand for *lifelong learning*[2]. In today's world, survival has come to mean participation in a ruthlessly competitive life game[3], while communities and societies have lost their sense of cohesion. Where job guarantee integrated and homogenised through (however unequal) distribution of a common fate that promised the daily bread within a stratified social body, lifelong learning reverses the normative priorities by deliberately debilitating employment prospects for the entire body politic. Even if it survives as a theoretical abstraction, the notion of *we* has perished under the fragmentation of individual intentions and possibilities. The permeating insecurity that affects all social classes is whitewashed as the objective integration of personal differences over which everyone is anyway individually responsible.[4]

What's more, this dis-integration is presented as inevitable. The game of educational socialisation is no more than a mere exercise for a life game with predetermined and non-negotiable rules. In a society where individual educational and professional conditions are completely separate from the collective's prosperity, everyone must think that their well-being is irrelevant to both their future and their past.[5] In order to be able to lift the weight of their personal responsibilities, people must have complete control over their own fate. Education thus becomes part of a wider procedure of inuring individuals to a ruthless and unsparing reality. Being instructed in the rules of life no longer is an exercise of participation in common values, nor an end in itself, nor an innocent activity[6]; neither is it just a game of chance. Imitating life, education appears a merciless competitive game[7] where everyone uses their relative advantage against everyone else. The importance of education for the production process cannot be found in its contribution to intellectual capital; education has instead become crucial because of the individualistic and competitive way it happens, and the institutionally assessed and recognised rewards it conveys. In other words, education has become another segment of production.[8]

In emerging knowledge societies, the old job-based social organisation is being replaced by forms of promoting and exploiting personal and private work-related knowledge, skills, and expertise. Thus, the value of labour force is no longer measured as an abstract figure; its evaluation is 'objective', and it happens on an individual basis, retrospectively, and singularly. The same thing happens during the learning process: the periodic assessment of academic performance is nothing more than a ceremonious rehearsal that anticipates the future employee's annual review process.

Thus, the ideological essence of lifelong learning becomes evident: people must become used to a volatile social place that has to be continually earned. Since they cannot know in advance the future needs of an increasingly unpredictable labour market, they also can't assume that education is *ever* complete. Access to knowledge becomes then just a wager[9] based on assessing one's own future necessity which, anyway, will only be temporary and potentially reversible. Like financial capital, human capital and individual expertise and knowledge are invested, managed, and rewarded within a whimsical and uncertain marketplace.

In this sense, the educational identity of people is also in a metastatic state.[10] Already from a young age, children must embrace the idea that their individual success depends on successfully playing an unpredictable game where their skills are constantly renewed and reviewed. The identification of learners and workers with their scholarly performance obeys the same logic: everything and everyone is subject to results-based evaluations. Education is organised on the principle of production maximisation. Instead of long-term work relationships that engaged actual people with a past, a present, and a future, we get impersonal, revocable, and opportunistic fixed-term contracts that apply to transferable and exploitable task completions. People must pay the price of betting on the outcome of their mandatory self-differentiation. *This* is the quintessential risk society.

The deregulation of age-old rhythms

The consequences are numerous: first, the symbolic weakening of primordial rituals of transition from prematurity to maturity. Let's remember that in earlier societies, the natural cohesion and solidarity of both primary kin units and wider communities and societies was substantiated on the basis of universal expressions of differentiation amongst children, adolescents[11], students, workers, disabled people, the retired, and so on. The social semantics attached to these transitions have always been considered natural and frictionless[12]—maybe because the succession of generations allowed lived time to be harmonised with a sense of participation in the otherwise incomprehensible cosmic time. In this sense, the social and symbolic hierarchies of roles, responsibilities, and duties among successive age groups and, by extension, among groups of people distinguished on the basis of physical abilities or gender constituted a transhistorical constant. Now, the ideological and organisational instability of social roles within time will most definitely have disruptive socio-psychological consequences.

But there is something even more ominous happening. The widespread fetishisation of lifelong learning undermines not only the *organisational* but also the *biological* preconditions of educational undertakings. In spite of technocratic assertions, learning incapacitation always comes earlier than expected. Whilst every youth is capable of learning to speak Chinese, play the violin, or master algebra, very few adults can sufficiently attain these skills. From a certain point onwards, the onset of mental sclerosis, psychological fatigue, and the difficulty of absorbing new information, combined with increasing family obligations and, crucially, the weight of past failures and disappointments all make adaptability much harder and stressful.[13] In this regard, lifelong learning could even be considered inefficient and counterproductive.

Ultimately, however, all of this matters little, because the sort of lifelong learning that is not offered together with the lifelong provision of education as an unquestionable cultural end in itself, available to everyone indiscriminately, is neither autonomous nor democratic; it remains captive to the all-too-familiar developmental agenda. And, even as such, its use is quite limited: against its apologists, it is not able to decisively enrich the collective knowledge reserves, nor does it disturb the terms of labour distribution within society by re-educating and reincorporating weakened and discouraged members into the workforce. After all, in times of downsizing and of increasing professional uncertainty, such a prospect would automatically transfer a large share of the unemployment to the young. Still, although the results of an education that is provided during an entire lifespan are, as we have seen, questionable, the ideological and political reverberations of its dominance remain undiminished. In societies that are bent on competing with soaring uncertainty in their workforce, the hype around lifelong learning provides the perfect ideological alibi: when access to self-improvement and self-differentiation is offered to everyone equally and in all stages of their (professional) life, nobody has the right to protest. Individual responsibility is elevated to a constant and unyielding strategic rule of survival for everyone, at any moment, and at all ages.

Those that the system discards, the unlucky ones, those that haven't prudently secured their old age, those that are not able to learn new tricks, and those finally defeated in this struggle for survival have no one to blame but their own carelessness, their misfortune[14], or their incompetence. They are not perceived as the victims of an unfair society or of their damn luck—but as deserving sufferers of their personal deficiencies. Even, then, if it does not correspond to some Hobbesian *human nature*, the war of all against all seems nowadays firmly planted as an unquestionably rational—and therefore inviolable—rule of social coexistence. It is considered not only natural and inevitable, but also politically and morally correct that anyone who does not act like the proverbial industrious mouse should end up like the lazy one. In stark contrast to the jobless of the past who, thinking that they might be poor victims of the market, could still hope for—and claim—social support, today's unemployables are not only stigmatised as useless, but also *self*-stigmatised as unworthy of institutional protection.[15] Citizens who could until recently enjoy some semblance of solidarity with their dignity intact have overnight been transformed to loathsome beggars. Failure and poverty arouse feelings of shame and guilt.[16]

The new biopolitical self-discipline

The ideological individualisation of the socialisation process must be seen in this light: free people, forced to exploit all available opportunities that might improve their station in the competitive game— and, thus, come into potential conflict with all their compatriots—will henceforth be forced to invent, plan, and promote their individual strategies and the specifics of their socialisation and re-socialisation by minimising individual risks and uncertainties.[17] Being owed nothing, they also have no debt to anyone.[18] In this profound privati-sation of competitive rules and regulations, explicit external control is giving its way to the biopolitical self-discipline and self-acclimatisation of useful and versatile minds.[19] Being responsible for plan-ning its personal future and organising its con-stantly assessed usefulness, today's and tomorrow's workforce is asked to willingly conform to the mer-ciless rules of the competitive game.

People are no longer socialised as aspiring mem-bers of a collective. From an early age, they are told to function as competitive players who must seek, by and for themselves, their own 'authentic' cultural and practical truth. At the same time, they are also indoctrinated in the idea that "we are dif-ference, that our reason is the difference of dis-courses, our history the difference of times, our selves the difference of masks. That difference, far from being the forgotten and recovered origin, is this dispersion that we are and make".[20] With the risk of social death hanging over their heads, they are taught to experience difference as a choice that life has made them make. Those who will not suc-cessfully self-differentiate must prepare to pay the price. Personal failure will be interpreted as the *objective* result of an irrational—therefore shame-ful—ideological and moral insubordination[21].

For now, the logical and ideological circle seems to be closing: a social setting that neither explicitly compels nor supports does not expect commitment. Individuals are exclusively in charge of their personal strategic choices. And, in the context of mass pluralistic *societies of spectacle*[22], choices are more abundant in alternative meanings, opportunistic fantasies, and thematic diversity than ever before. Everyone is able, entitled, and obliged to decide their game plan, their personality, their different and personalised identity—and, by the same token, their alibi and their hideaway. If, in its dynamic potential, this decision is merciless, it is also frenzied—in the end, instrumental realism slips into a kind of surrealism:

> We are the Free Men and this is our Corporal. – Three cheers for freedom, rah, rah, rah! We are free. – Let's not forget, it's our duty to be free. Hey! not so fast, or we might arrive on time. Freedom means never arriving on time – never, never ! – for our freedom drills. Let's disobey together . . . No! not together: one, two, three! the first will disobey on the count of one, the second on two, the third on three. That makes all the difference. Let's each march out of step with the other two, however exhausting it may be to keep it up. Let's disobey individually – here comes the corporal of the Free Men![23]

7

HISTORY
Gets the Last and Longest Laugh

Globalisation has changed the way we understand survival and life. Having to make more decisions than we need or can afford to, manage more crises than we can handle, and experiment with more alternatives than we could ever comprehend, we persevere by resorting to fantasies. As always, it's ideas about human nature that determine the reality of our existence. The inherent and inalienable sense of dignity that autonomy provides, even if it cannot fully satisfy one's sense of *being* and cannot be expressed but as a tautology, nonetheless seems to be the necessary semantic and normative prerequisite of an independent and conscientious *well*-being. By elevating man's untameable life-giving spirit above the crass material reality that keeps him alive, liberal humanism continues unimpeded in its enduring rationalising course.

But there is nothing odd about that. As we have seen, just as states, nations, and societies are weakened, so too are the concepts of shared space and time, shared normative origins, shared destiny, and shared cultural *mythoi*; we are compelled to face life as one against all. We are bombarded with an overwhelming number of options amongst infinite, and often irreconcilable, signals and symbols, messages and incentives. The 'promise' of flexibility concerns not just the market's operation, the structure of work contracts, or the conditions of survival; faced with an ever-changing reality, *all* expressions of rational individual action must be perceived and systematised as provisional, adaptable, flexible. The consecration of freedom of choice does not refer then just to the weakening of external ties. It could potentially also result in freeing individuals from semantic patterns, identities, and traditions. When meanings, values, certainties, and the primordial symbols of space are in retreat, everyone becomes responsible for choosing their personal signals and symbols and for devising their own illusions and chimeras. If Lévi-Strauss was right that "whoever says 'Man', says 'Language', and whoever says 'Language', says 'Society'"[1], then the mandatorily self-differentiated individuals of our times are led to believe (boast, even) that they can speak their own symbolic language, give meaning to their own society, devise their own culture, choose independently and autonomously their own myths, and think up their own strategies.

Freedom of choice does not concern everyone equally, however, and precisely this is the political significance of the present inquiry around alterity. Indeed, regardless of how pleasantly enriching the promotion of cultural autonomy sounds, and how the right to recognition contributes to moral tolerance and ideological democratisation, these ideas can't flourish in a societal void. It is anything but surprising that they are thriving during times when social rights and collective symbolic havens have first been depleted. The issue of their *actual* effects and side effects on the organisation of everyday social relations remains effectively unaddressed and unresolved.

Regardless of its underlying logic, the recognition of individual cultural autonomy seems to replace, ennoble, and dignify survivalist and biostrategic uncertainty and heteronomy. In order to offset the weakening of collective expectations and pursuits, alterity is further imprisoning individuals in their privacy.[2] The fetishised reflection of free individuals is projected as a self-sufficient vision, whilst the burning issue of their *actual* sustenance—without which all identities and alterities are pointless luxuries—is swept under the carpet.

It seems that age-old normative hierarchies are being reversed. The fact itself that cultural choice appears equally as—or perhaps more—pressing, urgent, and inescapable as the material needs that guarantee survival has important ideological implications. From the moment that it is accepted that people are not allowed to survive unless they willingly and responsibly plan their own productive alterity, life is subordinated to the ruthless laws of market economy. This reeks of merciless nineteenth-century social Darwinism where, to paraphrase Herbert Spencer, those who cannot live are better off dead. To add to that, people are nowadays expected not just to *comply with*, but to *wholeheartedly endorse* the common wisdom of their times. That is to say, free individuals are not forced to simply capitulate to the inflexible laws of natural selection; they must also respect, worship, and use them to their advantage.

This might explain why the discourse around difference and cultural identity flourished mainly in academic circles and affluent Anglo-Saxon middle classes. Even if alterity movements are not literally bourgeois, they are still unbothered by the problems of those who are altogether excluded from society.[3] Emancipatory will is by definition confined to a given system of social relations and inequalities. Unsurprisingly, then, references to abstract natural human decency, pursuit of cultural autonomy, and promotion of the right to difference seem to neither concern nor inspire the masses of workers; less so the unprotected illegal, marginalised, homeless, stateless, useless, non-employable, destitute people forced to live and survive outside society. These people, to quote Giorgio Agamben, not being citizens with rights, have no *bio* (political life), but are merely focused on their *zoe* (naked life).[4] They have no motive—or reason—to be concerned with their human nature, to claim their right to difference, or to realise their collective cultural identity; not more so, anyway, than securing their survival.[5] Cultural autonomy is the concern of those who are *already* incorporated in established social hierarchies; those, namely, who, not being chained to poverty, can worry about problems arising from the Other's gaze.

The unquestioned furtherance of the cultural difference agenda helps muffle all non-cultural differences and inequalities. It is, indeed, telling that demands for respect and recognition of cultural particularities are rarely voiced in terms of, or together with, demands for relieving systemic exploitation and misery. The socio-economic inequality of market societies is considered inevitable, reasonable even. The fetishisation of individual liberty means accepting the equality of all before their responsible alterity, but not before the terms of their survival. In this sense, even if people appear equal before their choices, cultural demands concern mostly those who are *more* equal than others. The rest, like Derrida said, are mere observers: like animals, they can do nothing acceptable to secure their livelihood, they are at the same time morally accountable *and* ontologically absolved.

Even, then, if it is well-intentioned, the push for recognising rights to difference appears in many respects morally corrupt and politically ambiguous. On the one hand, it helps clean up nationalistic and racist bigotry from political rationalisation, thus promoting the never-ending project of the Enlightenment.[7] But, on the other, it covers up the physical and ideological subjugation of ever more people to a system that deprives them of any possibility of survival.[8] Even if it is not consciously used as an alibi or as justification for the disappearance of political discourse from the fields of real power, economy[9], and class-constituted society, the discourse around free cultural alterity is at best mystifying—at worst, deceptive. Like Adorno emphasized,

> Where freedom appears as a motive in political stories today, as for example in the praise of heroic resistance, it has the shameful quality of a powerless reassurance. The outcome always ends up being determined by world politics, and freedom itself emerges as ideological, as a speech about freedom, with stereotypical declamations.[10]

Reversibility of social cohesion

In the same vein, the concept of social cohesion is also undergoing similar changes. Social cohesion is neither obvious nor transhistorical. Strictly speaking, it can only be developed when the terms pertaining to the internal consolidation of the whole can potentially be questioned; namely, when the latter's reproduction is at stake. Therefore, these issues could never be raised in the big and permissive premodern dynastic and religious societies, nor within smaller communities, groups, and families. Such social entities were reproduced more or less automatically, through systems of symbolic exchange rooted in all-too-potent unconscious mental structures[11] that gave meaning to the codes of interpersonal mutuality. It should not surprise us that in almost all premodern societies, reciprocity in general and the practice of exchanging gifts specifically were fundamental social practices, the epicentre of informal but binding rules.[12] In social formations that were termed and functioned as holistic, mutuality and rationalistic selfishness[13], solidarity and aggression, behavioural reflexes and reflective planning could coexist and converse. In this context, the relationship between individual and collective remained open and unsystematised. This is why the citizenry's compliance to the rules of symbolic exchange were treated as a duty not only towards particular recipients but towards the entire collective. The question of cohesion appeared, thus, as concomitant with the question of society itself; a non-cohesive society is a contradiction in terms.

Modernity changed all that. The dominance of capitalist relations and the consolidation of the rule of law meant that independent legislating and the impersonal and free market would undo all traditional mutualities and internalised regulatory reflexes. The self-serving economic person's individualism[14], sealing the passage from the age of the sovereign state to the age of convention[15], penetrated all social relations[16]. The moment a society made of free individuals became incapable of inventing mechanisms that would guarantee its perpetuation, preserving the current state of affairs turned into a crucial matter. As a result, the issue of social cohesion was posited at the centre of new political enquiries.

This is what makes collective identities that were constructed inside national powers historically significant. The intermediation of the nation placed the issue of the now-essential social cohesion at the epicentre of the new collective imaginary. Counterbalancing the troublesome individualistic tendencies, common identities appeared as an omnipresent and multivalent social glue that made the individual's symbolic identification with the wider group, the continuation of duties towards imaginary totalities, and the birth of a new national solidarity possible. And this, in an age of radical reshuffling of national collective identities, provided a historically necessary counter-entropic force.

The process of symbolic homogenisation was however not enough. Consolidating the social state and instituting social rights required that the imaginary and ideological coherence of nation-states be expanded. By incorporating citizens in constituted networks of solidarity, by assuming specific responsibilities towards them, and by idealising the state's pastoral role, the unity of concrete societies was strengthened. In this light, the state-as-shepherd appeared as a new network of unassailable normative mutualities and symbolic exchanges. Thus, going beyond its righteous and logical origins, the social contract itself was rebranded as a vague *but symbolically indispensable* contract with the people. In the name of common welfare, people's compliance to the general social and legal commitments was accompanied by the (explicit or unvoiced) promise—or at least expectation—that their present and future survival and prosperity would be safeguarded. Regardless of how people thought about, organised, and planned their life, they were from the outset integrated in a network of general mutuality. After all, the demand for social cohesion and solidarity concerns everyone equally: the rich *and* the poor, the unfortunate *and* the fortunate, the skilful *and* the unqualified, the prudent *and* the careless.

Even more so since—exactly like it was the case in premodern societies—the symbolic potency of instituted mutuality, unbalanced support, implicit duties, and social solidarity in social states all have to go beyond particular transactions between private and free individuals. The range of symbolic exchanges concerns a (timeless) society in its entirety. And, for this reason, the relation between the flock and the shepherd—between individuals and the whole—cannot be conceived *ad hoc*, or within specific circumstances conventionally determined by predefined temporal and functional needs.[17] As a structurally self-evident moral necessity, solidarity is perceived in the context of a social happening that must remain open and indeterminate.[18] The symbolic ties that connect a continuous society with transitory individuals are constant and eternal. Regardless of their individual wishes and specific needs, *all* citizens participate *ex officio* in a single cohesive and organised net of symbolic and material mutualities. Timeless homogeneous provenance and timeless solidarity are formulated on a single imaginary construct. The moral contract with the people and the substantiation of the nation appear as historical equivalents.

One of the perhaps most crucial expressions of the social state's historical sway is that it appeared able to stir hope that a named and delineated society would (again) be possible to be reproduced indefinitely through almost automatic and macroscopically self-evident consensual procedures. And from the moment that social cohesion could be forever guaranteed in predetermined ways and with consensual procedures, it was reasonable to assume that resistance to the forces of entropy would remain forever effective.[19] For the first time, most, if not all, citizens could believe that contributing to a solid and palpable social cohesion and solidarity is to their advantage. The self-interested individual appeared finally reconcilable with the substantiated collective. Regarding the terms of civic consensus, an *end of history* was already beginning to show.

But things turned out differently. As it later became apparent, the historical and financial viability of an inherently unstable marriage between liberal procedural justice of the rule of law and actual solidary justice of the interventional social state[20] remained delicate. The political and ideological consequences of this change were profound. With the counter-attack of neoliberalism, the decay of European social democracies, and the enfeeblement of sealed national spaces, the issue of social cohesion seemed to be surpassed by being *by*passed. It is not surprising to see that the age-old demands for social solidarity were allowed to collide with a thoroughly unashamed individualism. If we concede that it is impossible to impose on people a sense of mutuality and a list of duties not *explicitly* sanctioned by law and not *freely* chosen by them and, consequently, that no one can claim anything they are not absolutely entitled to, then the issue of solidarity falls prey to particular situations and conjunctures.

As a result, the demands for mutuality and solidarity could no longer be articulated as essential, instituted or not, collective prerequisites. Precisely this is the crux of another remarkable transformation: the issue of solidarity has indeed been transposed to the field of individual moral, cultural, or political *preferences*. To the extent that each person is individually responsible for and in charge of their survival, they are also exclusively responsible for and in charge of their normative realisation.[21] Even if *man does not live on bread alone*, anything that falls beyond sustenance concerns only him. Everyone is summoned to freely and responsibly balance the books between their own selfishness and their altruism. From the moment that social relations can be reproduced unchanged, mutuality becomes redundant and solidarity privatised—and so both can be reduced to polite and discretionary requests. After a century, the *social issue* is again hanging over a moral and political void.

Dead ends and tautologies

Based on the above, it cannot be a coincidence that in our radically 'de-compulsoralised' societies, the motivational instructions "Be free!", "Be different!", "Be yourself!", "Write your own story!", "Take control of your life!", etc. neither have nor pretend to have specific normative content. Having apparently been weaned off their Kantian preconditions, they constitute generic strategic rationalisations. And at the same time, they appear like irresolvable double binds[22] not far removed from the sort of empty (rhetorical) injunctions like "Be impulsive!", "Be original!", or even the self-contradicting "Don't obey rules!". In a certainly interesting way, widespread compliance with such prescriptions would in fact only annul them. In a competitive world where all games are zero-sum, individual differentiation for the purpose of surviving or becoming emancipated would be as pointless as everyone trying to get a better view by standing on their toes at the same time.[23] This, nonetheless, is irrelevant. In our brave new world, it matters very little that, whilst everyone is expected to toil more and move faster, no one knows in advance whether this extra effort will yield any measurable or desirable results. The most anyone can hope for is that, like Lewis Carroll's Black Queen, if they run as fast as they can, they might remain stationary.

This perfectly captures the essence of the current re-signification of the world. The fetishisation of self-differentiation implies that, responsible for their identity and social function as individuals are, they will forever remain able and willing to blame themselves for the woes that befall them. By intervening in the order of ideas and inventing new words, powers readjust the social conditions of their reproduction. It is not accidental that all the grand, albeit vague[24], normative origins of the modern world are losing their dangerously motivational content. The substitution of grand injunctions with their instrumental cousins doesn't highlight the continuity but, rather, marks the ultimate break with the subversive vision of perpetual emancipation.[25] If progress is replaced by development, freedom by the right to difference, equality by equal opportunities, justice by lenience and equity, welfare by handouts, fraternity by private support networks, etc., then the ideas expressed in the Enlightenment vernacular and materialised by civic modernity are defused and de-substantialised. That's reasonable. Derrida said it: the first thing a conqueror does is rename.

In this spirit, our age's widespread despair is not merely material, but moral and intellectual too. Weak powers need small words and controlled despairs. If Goethe was right that it is only in the face of despair that we see hope, this hope cannot but become distant when, having lost faith in common normative ideals, desperate individuals are led to futile introspection about their personal shame and guilt. To the degree that by deciding on the object of their unfree alterity, these destitute people set in motion forces in their life and in the lives of others that cannot be reversed, even if they change their mind, "their moment of freedom was yesterday"[26]. It looks like all the forms of intrinsically dangerous utopian thoughts are weakened. When the Blochian *something which does not yet exist* can be fragmented into the inexperience of individual hopes, expectations, chimeras, and rationalisations, illusions about changing the world can all hide behind the deceptive promise of changing just individual selves. The compulsively self-differentiated remain equally, and possibly more, imprisoned than the compliant. And, much more crucially, they can no longer pursue anything together with others. Nowadays, Schiller's *Ode to Joy* speaks not to the millions, but to each person separately.

Changes in the terms of appropriating the relation between each individual and everyone else are, therefore, all too important. If Rousseau's realisation, that people are forced to compare with each other[27], continues to set the wider context inside which the competitive game of facing mirrors is played, then people now appear additionally obliged (under penalty of their life's degradation) to plan their survival through the unconditional, constant, and in the final analysis irrelevant, strategic promotion of their individually differentiated qualities. Sartre's *hell is other people* acquires its specific historical content from the moment that someone cannot survive any other way than by imitating the need of others to differentiate themselves at any price.[28]

In this sense, idealising the right to difference whilst avoiding the discussion over material preconditions of man's survival suits well the established power orthodoxies. Pursuing a cultural autonomy that only needs to be crystallised conceptually, whilst setting aside the ruthless callings of survival heteronomy, remains a purely ideological and grossly hypocritical endeavour. Respect for otherness and equal recognition of the weak, the humble, and the abject would make some universally emancipatory sense *only* if the opening up of opportunities, symbolic goods, and fantasies was accompanied by a redistribution of the material preconditions for survival.[29] Since, however, the space of freedom is determined exclusively and negatively by providing symbolic and ideological opportunities to people so that they can think for and express themselves without external pressure, dignity becomes detached from material life.[30] As a result, the normative constitution of society loses its primordial moral content and, in the name of alterity, inequality and injustice can reign supreme.

Even more so since, by accepting without protest exclusive responsibility for a differentiation that might lead to salvation in this life, people are asked to make peace with both their strategic self-sufficiency and introspection, and with the structural uncertainty of their survival. The organised social collective's expectations are limited to the reasonable demand for those procedural rules that allow the competitive game to be played indefinitely, blindly, impartially, and only superficially fairly. This, after all, is the main ideological consequence of equal opportunities: far from preventing, it actually legitimises the victimisation of outcasts. It is the perfect form of virtual equality, one where the democratic principle of the standard of living becomes increasingly distant. As it happened in the nineteenth century, the initial equivalence of free people is trapped inside the formal principles of a procedural rule of law[31] organised in a way that makes it possible to tolerate and sanctify, as well as guarantee the perpetuation of, inequality and unfairness. *Equal opportunities* are nothing but the cherry on the colourful liberal cake. Exceeding even Mandeville's rationalisation[32], the invisible hand of the free market is enhanced by the unassailable regulatory endorsements that it needed.

The idea of cultural self-determination not only completes the idea of (negative) individual liberty; it also signals the (positive) triumph of an ungovernable meta-ethical but moralistic individualism that is invited to establish, perpetuate, and legitimise relations, differences, and hierarchies between people. Having finally defeated its ideological and political opponents, the strictly procedural perception of justice and fairness which had subsided in the face of the declining post-war welfare state is making a loud comeback. It is not surprising that the promised post-sovereign forms of identity[33] appeared during and were imposed within post-welfare, post-solidary, and post-emancipatory social rationalisations. In the name of procedural freedom and justice, and whilst the rich can safely hide behind a law and order that protects the supposedly impartial market environment (together with their rights and privileges), the final blow on the underprivileged has been dealt.[34]

History is far from done with irony. It seems certain that the major historical price of the recent consolidation of cultural tolerance is, at least under the current circumstances, the undeniable dominance of widespread, rampant, and moralised social analgesia. Even if the right to difference and the expansion and safeguarding of social guarantees and social rights are not in strict logical contrast with each other, but merely in historical conflict, the political and moral dilemmas remain open and complex. We obviously can't solve those. Perhaps, however, we can tread a path for a new understanding. Describing, like understanding, contributes to the universal happening and produces history. Anna Akhmatova wrote:

> During the frightening years of the Yezhov terror, I spent seventeen months waiting in prison queues in Leningrad. One day, somehow, someone 'picked me out'. On that occasion there was a woman standing behind me, her lips blue with cold, who, of course, had never in her life heard my name. Jolted out of the torpor characteristic of all of us, she said into my ear (everyone whispered there) – 'Could one ever describe this?' And I answered – 'I can.' It was then that something like a smile slid across what had previously been just a face.[35]

NOTES

Chapter 1

1. I couldn't possibly provide here a detailed account of the issues that surround the emergence of so-called *new social movements* and the proliferation of *cultural studies*. Indicatively, see Tracy B. Strong (ed.), *The Self and the Political Order* (Oxford: Blackwell, 1992), and Craig Calhoun (ed.), *Social Theory and the Politics of Identity* (Oxford: Blackwell, 1994). Charles Taylor's contributions made the issue of *recognition* an indispensable part of contemporary discourse that focuses on collective identities and differences. (See Charles Taylor, "The Politics of Recognition", in Charles Taylor et al., Amy Gutmann (ed.), *Multiculturalism: Examining the Politics of Recognition* (Princeton: Princeton University Press: 1994) and, by the same author, *Sources of the Self: The Making of the Modern Identity* (Cambridge: Cambridge University Press, 1992).

2. The debate over the protection of free individual cultural self-determination, the right to difference, and multiculturalism all fall under the same historical rubric: the augmentation of personal liberty, the institutional affirmation of freely constituted cultural

groups, and the new model of organising societies share the same conceptual starting point.

3. Hans-Georg Gadamer, *Reason in the Age of Science* (Cambridge, MA: MIT Press, 1982), 198.

4. See the works of Jean Baudrillard and Fredric Jameson.

5. Jean Baudrillard, *L'Échange impossible* (Paris: Galilée, 1999), 30.

6. Sigmund Freud, *Essais de psychanalyse* (Paris: Payot, 1989), 90.

7. Sigmund Freud, "On Narcissism, An Introduction", in *On Metapsychology: The Theory of Psychoanalysis: The Penguin Freud Library*, vol. 11 (Harmondsworth: Penguin, 1991), 67.

8. See Erich Fromm, *Fear of Freedom* (London: Routledge & Kegan Paul, 1960). For a different approach, see Ronald Dworkin, *Taking Rights Seriously* (London: Duckworth, 1977), 272.

9. See Richard Sennett, "Growth and Failure: The New Political Economy and its Culture", in Mike Featherstone and Scott Lash (eds.), *Spaces of Culture: City, Nation, World* (London: Sage, 1999), 14.

10. See Paul Ricœur, *Freud and Philosophy: An Essay on Interpretation* (New Haven & London: Yale University Press, 1970), 234.

11. This could be the meaning of Hegel's *freedom of the void*. See G. W. F. Hegel, "*Grundlinien der Philosophie des Rechts*", par. 5. See also Fredric Jameson, *The Seeds of Time* (New York: Columbia University Press,

1994), 35–36.

12. See Marcel Gauchet, *Le Désenchantement du monde: Une histoire politique de la religion* (Paris: Gallimard, 1985), 16–17.

Chapter 2

1. As Hannah Arendt demonstrated, all political theory since the seventeenth century (with the exception of Hobbes) focused on the issue of liberty. See Hannah Arendt, "Autorité, tyrannie et totalitarisme", in *Les Origines du totalitarisme: Eichmann à Jérusalem* (Paris: Collection Quarto, Gallimard, 2002), 883.

2. See Jean-Pierre Dupuy, *Introduction aux sciences sociales: Logique des phénomènes collectifs* (Paris: Ellipses, 1992).

3. *Society* as a neutrally descriptive term appeared for the first time in the eighteenth century. It's normal that sociology, the study of societies, followed.

4. For further analysis of the concept of *order* as a conceptual and political juxtaposition to natural *disorder*, see, amongst others, Zygmunt Bauman, "Modernity and Ambivalence", in Mike Featherstone (ed.), *Global Culture: Nationalism, Globalization and Modernity* (London: Sage, 1990), 161–162.

5. In this sense, contrary to Louis Dumont's stringent distinction between holistic and individualistic societies, the modern individualistic model is equally holistic with the ones it replaced. The ideologically

violent traditional and self-evident holistic societies gave their place to societies that were governed by the new rationalised and mediated forms of ideological subjugation to the demands of political and ideological homogeneity.

6. See, amongst others, Homi Bhabha, "DissemiNation: Time, Narrative and the Margins of the Modern Nation", in H. K. Bhabha (ed.), *Nation and Narration* (London: Routledge, 1990).

7. Ulrich Beck, *Risikogesellschaft: Auf dem Weg in eine andere Moderne* (Frankfurt/Main: Suhrkamp, 1986).

Chapter 3

1. Jean-Paul Sartre, *L'Être et le Néant: Essai d'ontologie phénoménologique* (Paris: Gallimard, 1943), 308.

2. For an analysis of Valéry's study of the *I*, see Giorgio Agamben, *La Puissance de la pensée: Essais et conférences* (Paris: Payot-Rivages, 2006), 82.

3. "The formula of identity is "A = A," not "A remains A." It does not assert the equality of two spatially or temporally distinct stages of A." (Walter Benjamin, "Theses on the Problem of Identity", in *Walter Benjamin: Selected Writings, 1: 1913-1926*, ed. M. Bullock and M. Jennings (Cambridge, MA: The Belknap Press of Harvard University Press, 1996), 76.

4. According to Michel Foucault, "the issue at hand is not to percolate universalia in history, but to sub-

ordinate history in a thought that rejects them" (my translation). See Michel Foucault, *Dits et écrits*, ed. Daniel Defert and François Ewald (Paris: Gallimard, 1994), 56.

5. See, for example, Marcel Mauss, "Une catégorie de l'esprit humain: la notion de personne celle de 'moi'" (1938), in *Sociologie et anthropologie* (Paris: PUF, 1950), 331–361. See also Jack Goody, *Renaissances: The One or the Many?* (Cambridge: Cambridge University Press, 2010), 14–16.

6. For this inherent paradox of the self, see Arnold H. Modell, *The Private Self* (Cambridge, MA: Harvard University Press, 1993), 3. See also Charles Taylor, *Sources of the Self: The Making of the Modern Identity* (Cambridge: Cambridge University Press, 1992), 175.

7. This is a problem that has occupied psychoanalytic theory since Freud's "The Ego and the Id", in *Complete Psychological Works of Sigmund Freud*, vol. XIX (London: Vintage, 2001), 17.

8. See Benedict Anderson's analysis in *Imagined Communities: Reflections on the Origin and Spread of Nationalism* (London: Verso, 1991).

9. See David Hume, *An Enquiry Concerning Human Understanding* (Indianapolis: Hackett Publishing Company, 1993), 28.

10. Gilles Deleuze and Félix Guattari, *Qu'est-ce que la philosophie?* (Paris: Minuit, 1991), 101. Pierre Bourdieu's (who borrowed the term *habitus*) and Norbert Elias's (who also made use of it) approach lead to

the same conclusions. See Pierre Bourdieu, *Le Sens pratique* (Paris: Minuit, 1980), 87. The same could be said of Michel Foucault's *dispositif.* (See the analysis by Paul Veyne, *Foucault: Sa pensée, sa personne* (Paris: Albin Michel, 2008), 173–174. See also Stephen Mennell, "The Formation of We-Images: A Process Theory", in Craig Calhoun (ed.), *Social Theory and the Politics of Identity* (Oxford: Blackwell, 1994), 178–179.

11. Paul Ricœur, "Individu et identité personelle", in Paul Veyne (dir.) et al., *Sur l'individu* (Paris: Seuil, 1987), 54.

12. See Sigmund Freud, *Totem and Taboo* (London: Routledge, 2001), 108.

13. Claude Lévi-Strauss, *L'Identité: Séminaire interdisciplinaire dirigé par Claude Lévi-Strauss* (Paris: PUF, 1983), 10.

14. Within this context we can consider the change in meaning of personal pronouns. Like Norbert Elias demonstrated, it is in modern societies that the *I* was structurally contrasted with *You, He,* and also with *We* for the first time. All premodern forms of diffusion and overlapping between individuals, others, and the group in which everyone belongs recede in favour of a constitutionally differentiating individualism. (Norbert Elias, *La Société des individus* (Paris: Fayard, 1991), 208, 250. See also Émile Benveniste, *Problèmes de linguistique générale* (Paris: Gallimard, 1966). Thus, the grasp and conceptualisation of the self is saturated in a tension between a constantly redefined *I,*

and everything outside it. The modern *I* amounts to the internalised habit of a constant and autonomous self-differentiation. This autonomy is produced in the form of a universally internalised truth—which might be the *only* truth one never loses sight of.

15. According to Louis Althusser's terminology, this is the function of the state's ideological mechanisms. See "Idéologie et appareils idéologiques d'État", in *Positions* (Paris: Éditions Sociales, 1976).

16. In this sense, what is defined as human nature is nothing else but the reflection of cultural norms dominant in a society. The question of whether it's possible to discern permanent behavioural patterns and forms of appropriating the unique self is, of course, legitimate and probably inevitable. And this is why it continues being central in discussions between anthropologists, philosophers, psychoanalysts, and recently, biogeneticists. At present, however, this question cannot be answered. The terms of articulation between nature and culture, between the inborn and the acquired, are hidden behind an irresolvable scientific veil that renders credible distinctions impossible. From the moment that the being is itself saturated in preconceptions about what this being is, all forms of human action and consciousness about selfhood, even if they have biogenetic origins, are necessarily expressed through the meanings that are *already* crystallised in the shape of those societies that produce them. Attempts at reading those meanings are therefore only partial and by definition

incomplete efforts to interpret interpretations. (Clifford Geertz, *The Interpretation of Cultures* (New York: Basic Books, 1973)). In this sense, the historical development of thoughts on human nature reveals very little about the nature itself. What it does, however, is tell us a lot about the society that nurtures those thoughts—every culture constructs the human nature that it 'deserves'.

17. The problem, of course, is not strictly logical. See A. J. Ayer, *Philosophical Essays* (London: Macmillan, 1954), 275.

18. See Terry Eagleton, *The Idea of Culture* (Oxford: Blackwell, 2000).

19. The most formidable attempt to resolve this contradiction is obviously attributed to Kant. See, for example, James Schmidt (ed.), *What is Enlightenment? Eighteenth-Century Answers and Twentieth-Century Questions* (Berkeley, Los Angeles, London: University of California Press, 1996). Despite their philosophical integrity, however, these reflections presuppose that an internalised moral self-limitation remains always possible. (See Slavoj Žižek, *The Sublime Object of Ideology* (London: Verso, 1989). See also the comments in Stathis Gourgouris, *Does Literature Think?: Literature as Theory for an Antimythical Era* (Stanford: Stanford University Press, 2003)).

20. Mentioned in Isaiah Berlin, *Four Essays on Liberty* (Oxford: Oxford University Press, 1969).

21. Paul Valéry, *Tel quel* (Paris: Gallimard, 1941), 85 (my translation).

22. See Sigmund Freud, *The Complete Introductory Lectures on Psychoanalysis* (New York: W. W. Norton & Company, 1966).

23. According to Henri Laborit, freedom can only be grasped through ignorance of the factors that make us act (Henri Laborit, *L'Éloge de la fuite* (Paris: Gallimard, 1976), 77).

24. William Blake, *Proverbs of Hell*, Plate 9.

25. This might be what the wise Roman lawmakers meant when they defined the right of ownership as a right of use *and* abuse: *ius utendi et abutendi*.

26. Jean-Jacques Rousseau, *The Social Contract* (New York: Cosimo, 2008).

27. It is not surprising that Hume, Rousseau, and, even more severely so, the American founding fathers insisted on the logical and moral self-sufficiency of a primordial consensus that can be constantly undermined by its own historical refutation or annulment. But it also cannot surprise us that these philosophical or logical discussions diminished (or, rather, disappeared) from the moment that the civic form of indirect representative democracy was organised as an established power. From then on, the possibility of voluntary retraction on behalf of free signatories was eliminated—or at least thwarted. This was one of the basic institutional and symbolic side-effects of adopting a constitution. The non-revisable articles protect not only the individual rights, but also the perpetual inviolability of the dominant constituted society.

28. For a historical account of the distinction between *metaphorical* and *metonymical* conceptual constructions and classifications, see, amongst others, Patrick Tort, *La Raison classificatoire: Quinze études* (Paris: Aubier, 1989), 539.

29. In this context, a new criterion that will allow modern political power to be reduced to a common, ostensibly meta-transcendental conceptual origin emerges. The idea of common provenance of a people (which is instituted as a right of blood) will be instituted as ideological precondition for a distinction in the name of which the dominant decisions will be made, the common good established, and the ontological community of governed subjects delineated. This is the institutional and ideological precondition of the differentially modern political racism. (See the works of Michel Foucault, *Il faut défendre la société: Cours au Collège de France, 1976* (Paris: Gallimard/Seuil, 1997) and Giorgio Agamben, *Le Règne et la Gloire, Homo sacer, II, 2* (Paris: Seuil, 2008), 124–127).

30. For further reading on this issue, see Ernst Kantorowicz, "Les Deux Corps du Roi", in *Œuvres* (Paris: Gallimard, Quarto, 2000), 802.

31. For this issue, see Αντώνης Λιάκος, *Πώς το παρελθόν γίνεται ιστορία* (Αθήνα: Πόλις, 2007).

32. Jürgen Habermas, *Eine Art Schadensabwicklung* (Frankfurt: Suhrkamp, 1987), S. 159 f.

33. The processes at work behind the creation of the European ideological and institutional particularity—

which contrasts the free individual with the dominant and ideologically concrete nation-state whole—are, obviously, countless. On the individual's side, this particularity is founded on the philosophical discussions that took place in the context of capitalistically developing societies during the Enlightenment. On the whole's side, however, matters are far more complex, and connected to the geopolitical coordinates of a competitive European political system where power balances have always been delicate. Similar forms of ideological uniformity were not necessary in places such as East Asia, where imperial China acted unfettered by the peripheral states. In the latter's case, the construction of an internal and exclusive national identity was probably futile: not being directly threatened, powers could be readily reproduced. (See Giovanni Arrighi, *Adam Smith à Pékin: Les promesses de la voie chinoise* (Paris: Max Milo, 2009), 390).

34. I'm using the formulation *thrown into* for Heidegger's *Verworfenheit*. See Martin Heidegger, *Sein und Zeit* (Tübingen: Max Niemeyer Verlag, 1960).

35. This issue is thoroughly discussed in Κωνσταντίνος Τσουκαλάς, *Η Εξουσία ως λαός και ως έθνος: Περιπέτειες σημασιών* (Αθήνα: Θεμέλιο, 1999).

36. See "Introduction: Inventing Traditions", in Eric Hobsbawm and Terence Ranger (eds.), *The Invention of Tradition* (Cambridge: Cambridge University Press, 1984), 1.

37. See David Hume, *An Enquiry Concerning*

Human Understanding (Indianapolis: Hackett Publishing Company, 1993). See also Maurice Halbwachs, *Les Cadres sociaux de la mémoire* (Paris: Albin Michel, 1994), 38–39.

38. Rousseau was first to note the decisive importance of education in the process of national civic birth which, in turn, triggers the emergence of patriotism.

39. See Claude Lévi-Strauss, *La Pensée sauvage* (Paris: Plon, 1962).

40. Karl Kraus, *Words in Verse*, vol. 1.

41. Jorge Luis Borges, "Tlön, Uqbar, Orbis Tertius".

42. See Paul Veyne, *L'Inventaire des différences: Leçon inaugurale au Collège de France* (Paris: Seuil, 1976), 62.

43. See Zygmunt Bauman, "Modernity and Ambivalence" in Mike Featherstone (ed.), *Global Culture: Nationalism, Globalization and Modernity* (London: Sage, 1990), 34.

44. In this context, we may also analyse the historical connection between national and religious identity, which is a modern version of the *cuius regio eius religio* in societies where religious and national consciousnesses remained largely intertwined. Full secularisation in the form of separation of Church and State produced homogenising results without creating unbearable fractures only because, and to the degree that, the symbolic dominance of religious identifications had already been undermined. In this respect, the French and the American Revolutions were based on the Enlightenment.

45. See Sigmund Freud, *L'Homme Moïse et la religion monothéiste* (Paris: Gallimard, 1948), 24.

46. Many anthropological studies have shown that the sense of belonging to a group and the representation of collective identities of its members are not always reducible to tangible cultural structures or choices. For this reason, these collective identities are frequently fluctuating. On this issue, see, amongst others, Edmund Leach, *Political Systems in Highland Burma: A Study of Kachin Social Structure* (London: Athlone Press, 1954) and Fredrik Barth (ed.), *Ethnic Groups and Boundaries: The Social Organization of Culture Difference* (Boston: Little, Brown, 1969).

47. There is an obvious correlation to the ancient city, which is understood as the primordial, evident, and natural form of collectivity within which all others acquire meaning. Modern European political culture does not refer to citizens that 'know each other', but to free individuals that can remain anonymous. It should be reminded that, according to Aristotle, the ideal city should be no larger than an area visible to each citizen, and the body politic should be such that each citizen can recognise all others. In order to be able to claim its unparalleled prestige, direct democracy must appear functionally visible, tangible, and, therefore, transparent.

48. The question of who are the signatories of the contract was addressed in discussions over land rights and blood rights. The fact that the answers which fi-

nally prevailed were mostly mixed shows the perplexity caused when pure logic has to converse with a wayward and irregular history.

49. In the same way that pre-existing ethnic groups can be distinguished from the nations within which they will later be appropriated, one can attempt a conceptual distinction between the pre-existing minority groups and the *ipso jure* minorities that will retrospectively be acknowledged and recognised.

50. This is also why the issue of recognition of an imaginary community as a minority can never obey rigid, logical, and consolidated normative qualifications. Since the element of a delineated territory is absent, and a part of the population does not feel incorporated in the single national community, the question of the scale on which a cultural group can—or is entitled to—be formed as a self-sufficient entity remains open. In the final analysis, the issue of recognising and guaranteeing the rights of minorities appears directly related to their historically fluctuating political sway and popularity. In the same sense that there have always been and still exist *failed nations* (those that never managed to articulate a national political and cultural proposal), there have always been and still exist 'castrated' minorities (those that were historically ineffective in attaining their institutional and ideological identity and recognition).

51. Regardless of its normative substantiation, the claim for recognition on behalf of various groups is

premised on the historical precedent of nominal recognition and ideological entrenchment of national and religious minorities as a logical and organisational precondition for the achievement of their political protection. Once again, the symbolic potency of words is striking. What is *named* appears as *known*, the known as *existing*, and the existing is endowed with normative qualities and proceeds to advance political claims limited by history and circumstance. It is worth recalling that something similar happens with the constitutional protection of religious freedoms of all known or recognised religions under a regime where there is a dominant or official religion. (On this issue, see, amongst others, Α. Ι. Σβώλου and Γ. Κ. Βλάχου, *Το Σύνταγμα της Ελλάδος: Ερμηνεία, ιστορία, συγκριτικόν δίκαιον,* Μέρος 1 (Αθήνα: Αθήναι, 1954), 42).

52. With the obvious exception of countries such as the USA, Canada, or Australia that were the product of mass colonisation.

53. See Nicos Poulantzas, *L'État, le pouvoir, le socialisme* (Paris: PUF, 1978).

Chapter 4

1. Per the term Jean-François Lyotard used.

2. For an analysis of the significance between symbolic middle points and their spatial representation, see Marcel Detienne, *The Masters of Truth in Archaic Greece* (New York: Zone Books, 1996). From this

perspective, the locations where warriors and old men would gather, the ancient agora, the political and religious offices, and modern capitals all play similar roles.

3. The same happens in what concerns new territorial conflicts, namely wars. (For this issue, see Κωνσταντίνος Τσουκαλάς, *Πόλεμος και ειρήνη: Μετά το τέλος της Ιστορίας* (Αθήνα: Καστανιώτης, 2006).

4. See Paul Virilio, *La Bombe informatique* (Paris: Galilée, 1998).

5. This is apparent in the emergence of territorial, spatial, and classificatory thresholds. While offshore tax havens function as no man's lands, the multiplying stateless migrants appear as 'no land's people'. As a result, the axiomatic modern link between a person and a particular place where legal powers are exercised, and the link between all constituted places and a body of people that legally inhabit it ceases to be regarded as a general rule of understanding the relationship between people and space. New warlords, vagrant thieves, vagabonds, and entertainers are appearing. Like it happened in the Middle Ages, the relation between man and his surroundings is again unpredictable, spontaneous, and coincidental.

6. In these terms, unclassifiable *threshold* phenomena have multiplied. Like Mary Douglas notes, together with taxonomic uncertainty, the normative robustness of limits and dividing lines is also weakened. As a result, all intermediate hybrid formations are treated as foreign, disruptive, and appalling abominations that

disturb the order of the world's meanings. (See Mary Douglas, *Purity and Danger: An Analysis of Concepts of Pollution and Taboo* (Harmondsworth: Penguin, 1970)).

7. Norbert Elias, *Time: An Essay* (Oxford: Blackwell, 1992), 69.

8. Michel de Certeau "Ce que Freud fait de l'histoire", in *L'Écriture de l'histoire* (Paris: Gallimard, 1975), 292.

9. Interestingly, an enquiry previously at the centre of political and scientific discussion has completely vanished. Together with the question of protecting the national economy, the debates over national developmental policies have also waned.

10. I'm borrowing the term from Deleuze and Guattari (Gilles Deleuze and Félix Guattari, *Mille plateaux: Capitalisme et schizophrénie* (Paris: Minuit, 1980), 434). The same term is often used by Michael Hardt and Antonio Negri in *Empire* (Cambridge, MA: Harvard University Press, 2000) and, more recently, Zygmunt Bauman.

11. Kostas Axelos, *Le Jeu du monde* (Paris: Minuit, 1969), 226–227.

12. Lately, the issue of trust has emerged as a major political and ideological concern. (The great Fukuyama recently abandoned his ended history and wrote a new bestseller, *Trust*). It's interesting to observe that the revival of this discourse—in moralistic terms, of course—coincides with the transformation of transactional

ethics in the direction of an increasing separation of rationalistic profitability from permanent consequences of actions. Indeed, the elevation of trustworthiness into an indispensable transactional (bourgeois) virtue can be identified with rationalism only to the extent that it goes hand in hand with the interests of the transactors. And this only happens to the extent that, through credibility and 'having a good name', future profitable transactions can be anticipated. In these terms, it's to everyone's advantage to be and appear honest.

13. See Pierre Rosanvallon, *Le Capitalisme utopique* (Paris: Seuil, 1989).

14. See, amongst others, Robert Castel, *Les Métamorphoses de la question sociale: Une chronique du salariat* (Paris: Fayard, 1995), 203–295.

15. For an analysis of the importance of permanent and direct social networks in the creation and reproduction of constant normative structures, see, amongst others, Robert Merton, *Social Theory and Social Structure* (New York: The Free Press, 1968), 211. From a different perspective, the same issue is treated by Werner Sombart in *Der Bourgeois* (München and Leipzig: Duncker & Humblot, 1913).

16. See, for example, David Harvey, *A Brief History of Neoliberalism* (Oxford: Oxford University Press, 2005), 178, where the different types of capital accumulation effected through direct dispossession of resources and wealth are analysed.

17. Walter Benjamin "On the Concept of History"

in *Walter Benjamin: Selected Writings, 4: 1938-1940*, ed. H. Eiland and M. Jennings (Cambridge, MA: The Belknap Press of Harvard University Press, 2003), 392.

18. This is thoroughly analysed in Κωνσταντίνος Τσουκαλάς, *Είδωλα πολιτισμού: Ελευθερία, ισότητα και αδελφότητα στη σύγχρονη πολιτεία* (Αθήνα: Θεμέλιο, 1998).

19. For further reading on this issue, see Κωνσταντίνος Τσουκαλάς, "Με τη σκέψη στο έργο του Νίκου Πουλαντζά: Για την ανασυγκρότηση μιας θεωρίας του καπιταλιστικού κράτους", in *Ελληνική Επιθεώρηση Πολιτικής Επιστήμης 32* (Dec. 2008), 7–25.

20. This might be a most representative symptom of the totalnormative degeneration of the independent critical thought of Enlightenment towards a prescribed, single-minded, and pre-systematised path. Like Cornelius Castoriadis noted, the finite Aristotelian entelechy was transubstantiated in the direction of Judaeo-Christian faith in the infinite nature of God and, by extension, of a world that can have no limits. (Cornelius Castoriadis, *Les Carrefours du labyrinthe: Domaines de l'homme* (Paris: Seuil, 1986), 138–143). It should not surprise us that the example was set by the messianic apologists of central planning in the socialist camp. Already from the 1920s, the five-year plans subordinated the qualitative and normative demand for *subversion of the relations of production* to the *development of productive forces*. In the presence of an absolute historicist confidence, these subversions can wait.

21. See Κωνσταντίνος Τσουκαλάς, "Πρόλογος", in Νορμπέρτο Μπόμπιο, *Δεξιά και Αριστερά: Σημασία και αίτια μια πολιτικής διάκρισης*, trans. Ελεονώρα Ανδρεδάκη (Αθήνα: Πόλις, 1995).

22. See Paul Baran, *The Political Economy of Growth* (New York: Monthly Review Press, 1957), 5.

23. See Amartya Sen (ed.), *Growth Ecomonics* (Harmondsworth: Penguin, 1970), 9–10. The repercussions of (temporary) historical insecurity of liberal camps will be readily accepted by mainstream thought. From the moment that the Soviets paved the way for the rationalisation of all socio-political utopias, the apologists of capitalist relations found themselves in familiar territory. From this perspective, it seems that the overzealous Stakhanov and the short-sighted, growth-obsessed technocrat are children of the same God. In other words, *more is more*.

24. The two terms (growth and expansion) were synonymous up to the 1970s. See Paul Samuelson, *Economics*, 10th ed. (New York: McGraw Hill, 1976), 725–726.

25. Again, the readiness with which this new paradigm was adopted is breathtaking. Indeed, although the issue of economic expansion exists in economic thought since Adam Smith, for more than a century it did not seem to concern anyone. See Mark Blaug, *Economic Theory in Retrospect* (Cambridge: Cambridge University Press, 1978), 701. And yet, within a few short years, it all of a sudden appeared in-

dispensable: see Joan Robinson, *Economic Philosophy* (Harmondsworth: Penguin, 1962), 94.

26. The sectors that were organised as legal, consolidated state monopolies are shrinking by the day. The deregulation of work relations signals the transformation of the workforce into yet another commodity; labour law as a special regulatory branch is vanishing; public works, transportation, communication, energy, water resources, as well as education, healthcare, pensions, and securities are all becoming either reciprocal or privatised; law and order and other sectors of governing are outsourced to private contractors; even justice (especially in the case of capitalist conglomerates) is assigned to private arbitration courts. The state remains responsible for legally coordinating the advancement of a general interest that is considered invariably to be at the mercy of market forces. After a fifty-year break, during which the exercise of power followed the prescriptions of an endogenous and autonomous *raison d'état*, liberalism imposed again its minimalistic rationale. Questions that examine the existence and activity of government power will thenceforth be answered based on the principle that government, actually or potentially, is itself an *excess*. See Michel Foucault, *Naissance de la biopolitique: Cours au Collège de France, 1978–1979* (Paris: Gallimard/Seuil, 2004), 325–327.

27. See Ulrich Beck, *Risikogesellschaft: Auf dem Weg in eine andere Moderne* (Frankfurt/Main: Suhrkamp, 1986).

28. See Alain Badiou, *Η πολιτική και η λογική του συμβάντος: Μπορούμε να στοχαστούμε την πολιτική;,* trans. Δ. Βεργέτης (Αθήνα: Πατάκης, 2008), 20.

29. See Giorgio Agamben, *Le Règne et la Gloire: Homo Sacer, II, 2* (Paris: Seuil, 2008), 17.

30. This issue is becoming increasingly pertinent in constitutional studies and political theory, partly in reference to the discretionary transference of sovereignty in the context of European integration.

31. Like postmodernism and post-Fordism, the term *post-sovereignty* betrays a certain conceptual bewilderment in the face of developments that challenge our certainties. After all, adding the prefix *post-* creates a new word without clearly defining its meaning.

32. See Carl Schmitt, *Political Theology: Four Chapters on the Concept of Sovereignty,* trans. George T. Schwab (Chicago: University of Chicago Press, 2005), 5. It should be noted that this much-celebrated opening sentence cannot accurately be translated from German. The German preposition *über,* which is rendered in English as *on,* refers both to the question of *when* there is a state of exception and to the issue of *how* it will be dealt with. Schmittian decisionism is simultaneously diagnostic and instrumentally and practically interventional.

33. Giorgio Agamben, *State of Exception,* trans. Kevin Attell (Chicago: University of Chicago Press, 2005).

34. This is institutionally sanctioned, too. The

discussion on the need for a constitutional reduction of the legitimate economic policies that would be the object of political decisions has started since the early 1980s. See, for example, Geoffrey Brennan and James Buchanan, *Monopoly in Money and Inflation* (London: Institute of Economic Affairs, 1981). A few years later, the Treaty of Maastricht was basically a ratification of Buchanan's suggestions: the state repudiates its control not only in exceptional circumstances, but also during normal times. Decisions are made by the European Central Bank, the International Monetary Fund, and mostly, the markets. Under these circumstances, the question of who is sovereign acquires a new twist.

35. See Michel Foucault, *Sécurité, Territoire, Population: Cours au Collège de France, 1977–1978* (Paris: Gallimard/Seuil, 2004), 110–111.

36. Michel Foucault, *Histoire de la sexualité I: La volonté de savoir* (Paris: Gallimard, 1976), 133.

37. In truth, the issue is far more complicated: the relations between political and financial power develop in the context of a historically evolving logic behind those two forms of power. Thus, taking into consideration the central importance of states, whilst the logic of political power is necessarily territorial and 'serial', the logic of capital accumulation is super-territorial and 'molecular'. (See David Harvey, *The New Imperialism* (Oxford: Oxford University Press, 2005), 26–27 and, by the same author, *The Enigma of Capital and the Crises of Capitalism* (London: Profile Books,

2010), 204–205. See also Giovanni Arrighi, *The Long Twentieth Century: Money, Power and the Origins of Our Times* (London: Verso, 1994). This, anyhow, should not be taken to mean that these two logics are entirely compatible. Even though in their long historical course they have coexisted, cooperated, and spread in the context of a constant osmosis between the powers that they serve, they can neither coincide nor ignore each other. If, then, it seems that we are amidst world-changing developments, this is partly owed to the fact that neither the transnational molecular capitals can completely rid themselves of the heavy shadow of political powers; nor can political powers move beyond, and regardless of the logic of, capital accumulation. The hidden perspectives of the battered U.S. hegemony and, even more so, the (unknown) dynamic of the Chinese state-controlled capitalism leave the issue of new forms of coarticulation between the territorial and the transnational logics hanging. Obviously, history hasn't yet played its hand.

38. Karl Marx, *Le 18 Brumaire de Louis Bonaparte* (Paris: Éditions Sociales, 1963), 56, 87.

39. Cornelius Castoriadis, *L'Institution imaginaire de la société* (Paris: Seuil, 1975).

40. Although what we today call *competition* tends to coexist with forms of social solidarity or social paternalism (see, for example, the typology suggested by János Kornai in *Contradictions and Dilemmas: Studies on the Socialist Economy and Society* (Cambridge, MA:

MIT Press, 1986), 54), we are for the first time witnessing the official and explicit rationalisation of the
necessity to favour the former over the latter.

41. The ideological charging of the word *bureaucracy*
is at the opposite end of Max Weber. What is ostensibly
the most rational organisational form is turned on its
head to express absolute incompetence. See the interesting analyses by Luc Boltanski and Éve Chiapello
in *Le Nouvel Esprit du capitalisme* (Paris: Gallimard,
1999).

42. See Zygmunt Bauman, *Living on Borrowed
Time: Conversations with Citlali Rovirosa-Madrazo*
(Cambridge: Polity Press, 2010), 39.

43. See Michel Foucault, "Omnes et singulatim:
Vers une critique de la raison politique", in *Le Débat*,
41 (Sept.–Nov. 1986), 5.

44. Although theory follows reality, it seems that it
also tries to contain it within idealistic and moralistic
formulations. Like in the case of rekindled interest
in trust (see above, Note 12), we are witnessing the
emergence of extensive scholarship focused on *free
riders*. Notably, this is happening at the same time
when the process of individualisation is reaching
its climax. Likewise, in relation to this new scourge
of liberal societies, the issue of political corruption
(See Κωνσταντίνος Τσουκαλάς and Τάκης Καφετζής
"Περί πολιτικής διαφθοράς", in *Ελληνική Επιθεώρηση
Πολιτικής Επιστήμης,* 31 (May 2008), 5–49). One
could claim that the social discourse is not focusing

on rational moral 'deviances' except when the social dynamic is threatening to turn them into rules.

45. Indeed, within only a few years, liberal capitalism seems to have broadened the scope of its ideological triumph. Following the historical fragmentation of the body politic into separate individuals-beneficiaries, it seems that the road has also been paved for the disturbance of *all* collective forms of action. Although as constitutionally sanctioned formations, trade unions, syndicalism, and strikes are still recognised as institutionally necessary, they are nonetheless subjected to increasing ideological devaluation and, from a certain point on, to sustained regulatory control. In the name of a common public 'developmental' concern and public developmental order, whilst the abusive furtherance of collective interests is subjected to intense administrative and judicial scrutiny, the separate trade demands are pushed into direct conflict with each other: a case of *divide and conquer*. Thus, the unanimous rhetorical renunciation of what is now detestable corporatism and of all so-called corporatist behaviours and formations (which are, after all, very hard to distinguish from all other forms of labour movements) should not come as a surprise. Once again, what is interesting is the eagerness to upend all the traditional normative prescriptions of words and ideas. We must keep in mind that just thirty years ago, the thriving European social democracy had assumed that corporatism—as an instituted form of mediation between opposed class interests—offered

a permanent organisational matrix for negotiation and resolution (under the watchful eye of the state) of differences between employers and workers. This tripartite consensual settlement appeared actually to be blocking the way to irrational social and class tensions. And, according to the leading scholar of corporatism, Philippe Schmitter, its star was just rising.

History proved again how crafty it can be: nothing should be considered definitively and irrevocably settled. As the recent case of Greece and the IMF's involvement show, despite the all-powerful constitutional, historical, and symbolic bastions that secure labour movements, a similar fate is in store for trade unionism. Events are taking place as if, ideally, the fragmented and individualised workers should never again be in a position to collectively negotiate and demand. Although monopolies and cartels are in full swing, the order of the day is: absolute and limitless fair competition between those that hold the same place in the production process (and this is especially applied in the case of workers).

46. Since 1999, the transposition of legitimating rationalisations has been severe. It is not surprising that *equal opportunities* dominated the discourse of Third Way politics between Clinton, Blair, Jospin, D'Alema, Cardoso, and Simitis—prompted by Ronald Dworkin's paper "Does Equality Matter?", in *Progressive Governance for the 21st Century* (Florence: Nov. 1999).

47. Bauman raises the issue of the historically

determined dialectic between safety and security, noting that the fetishisation of order and safety functions, amongst other concerns, as an ideological and symbolic substitute for widespread social insecurity and uncertainty (See Zygmunt Bauman, *Globalisation: The Human Consequences* (Cambridge: Polity Press, 1998), 117–120).

Chapter 5

1. According to René Girard, modern societies already from their onset exhibited a tendency to temper restrictions on desire. Together with abolishing the stratification of individuals, the compulsion to regulate their behaviours has also waned. This is the anthropological foundation of the expansion of opportunities of simulation amongst people, and the wider permeation of the fields of social antagonism between them. (See René Girard, *Des choses cachées depuis la fondation du monde* (Paris: Bernard Grasset, 1978), 401–406).

2. I can't possibly elaborate here on the concept and definition of *culture*. It would, anyway, be pointless, since what concerns us here is the word's social meaning and its use in political terms.

3. In these new coordinates, even the most fundamental taxonomic categories will shift. In the liberal distinction between public and private, and state and society, a new one will be added: between the organised society and its culture. As already separate from the

world of the free market, employment, and individual survival, the public space substantiated around the understanding and implementation of state power will be conceptually detached from a *literal* culture which lies beyond the public sphere of politics. Therefore, the fields of survival, of the contractually structured legitimate civic organisation, and of political expression tend to be crystallised conceptually in the form of ontologically distinct practices. Being functionally differentiated, social spheres will be formed as conceptually weatherproof from each other and will acquire different degrees of urgency. While the rational, economical, labour, and survival practices are urged to converge towards objectively rational maximisational market models, and political practices are unfolding within a committing (as far as the institutional and legal prescriptions go) political order, so too are cultural practices considered free choices. Man depends for his survival on the inevitable rules that are produced by the objective utilitarian discourse, and is subjected to the laws of the contractual polity—but, nonetheless, chooses freely his cultural references and actions. The sphere of culture and its distinction from both the private market/financial and the public will be designated in residual terms: what, in other words, *remains* after rational/survival and organisational/civil practices are deducted. (On this new *residual* understanding of culture, in contrast to *necessary* social practices, see Constantine Tsoucalas, "The Antinomies of 'Instrumental Culturalism'", in

Manwoo Lee (ed.), *Culture and Development in a New Era and in a Transforming World* (Seoul: Kyungnam University / UNESCO, 1994), 63). Therefore, regardless of the range of action that it covers, culture's free space is identified with that which remains unregulated; in other words, with whatever does not fall within the necessary (regulated) productive and cohabitational/political relations. Separated and absolved of the necessary and binding prescriptions of survival and cohabitation, culture is invested with whatever relates to the symbolic diversification and enrichment of life with values, meanings, and pleasures. It is in this context that ideas about the favoured and fetishised individual identity will be incorporated. Against (or, as an offset to) other commitments, free individuals are allowed to choose autonomously and rationally their difference, their cultural identity, and their cultural practices. Culture is elevated to the symbolic privileged space of expression, exercise, and cultivation of individual liberty.

4. The logical and practical impasse of an absolute and pure multicultural tolerance is no different from the institutional deadlocks of absolute democracy. The legal and institutional problem that arises when legitimate democracy has to deal with ideas and activities that deny or undermine democratic principles is no different from the problem of dealing with cultural phenomena and actions that conflict with the prevailing multicultural (or pancultural) model of socio-political organisation.

5. In keeping with the terminology introduced by Isaiah Berlin, one could speak of enrichment of negative liberty with ever more potent doses of positive liberty that attempt to answer the question of *who decides what I should and should not do or be.* (See Isaiah Berlin, *Four Essays on Liberty* (Oxford: Oxford University Press, 1969).

6. Gilles Deleuze, *Différence et répétition* (Paris: PUF, 1968), 280.

7. See Erving Goffman, *Stigma: Notes on the Management of Spoiled Identity* (Englewood Cliffs: Prentice-Hall, 1963).

8. See Chapter 3, page 23.

9. See Max Weber, *Rechtssoziologie* (Neuwied: Luchterhand Verlag, 1967), 69.

10. See Charles Taylor et al., Amy Gutmann (ed.), *Multiculturalism: Examining the Politics of Recognition* (Princeton: Princeton University Press: 1994).

11. See the remarks by Michael Walzer in Charles Taylor, Ibid., 99.

12. See, amongst others, "Introduction" in Tracy B. Strong (ed.), *The Self and the Political Order* (Oxford: Blackwell, 1992), 2.

13. The distinction between what is allowed and what is forbidden is historical. Regardless of how or why they were instituted, cultural prohibitions on cannibalism, adultery, polygamy, incest, homosexuality, drug abuse, nudity, transfusion, organ transplant, or wearing the chador are opposed to the idea of cultural autonomy.

In reality, the historicity of regulatory interventions is inherent in social cohabitation and organisation. This is the universal function of all 'innocent' and often unfathomable social prohibitions that become *taboos*. (See Sigmund Freud, *Totem and Taboo* (London: Routledge, 2001), 22).

14. See Michel Foucault's "Introduction" to Georges Canguilhem, *The Normal and the Pathological*, trans. Carolyn R. Fawcett and Robert S. Cohen (New York: Zone Books, 1991).

15. Matters get progressively complicated when demands for recognition extend to demands that presuppose specific material, organisational, or financial actions on behalf of the state. Thus, even if it is agreed that public educational and communicational ideological mechanisms (the radio, television) must facilitate and protect the cultural and linguistic particularities of cultural groups, the question of which groups deserve to claim this recognition and protection remains unanswered. Obviously, it is politically and financially impossible to provide education in all languages and dialects, regardless of practical, symbolic, and political considerations. There are indeed great differences between the French-speaking population of Québec, the Turkish-speaking population of Thrace, the remaining enthusiasts of Esperanto, or the few Icelanders. But the criteria that distinguish between the positively protected and the negligible cultural differences can neither be rational nor reducible to normative standards. They

remain *de facto* historical and political. Ultimately, only those cultural groups that can make enough democratic noise stand a chance of being recognised and protected.

16. Sigmund Freud, *Das Unbehagen in der Kultur* (Wien: Verlag, 1930).

17. In most premodern societies, common decisions were made through a *ritual of consensus* that amplified the symbolic bind of regulations. Neoliberal *rituals of democratic dissent* tempered but did not completely eradicate the creature of general consent (See Pierre Rosanvallon, *La Légitimité démocratique: Impartialité, réflexivité, proximité* (Paris: Seuil, 2008), 193). It could be argued that current developments reverse this reasoning: everything is taking place as if the creature of a consensual social contract can only be kept alive on the condition that it remains exempt from as many fields of social action as possible.

18. In reality, at the level of transgenerational reproduction of human beings, the institution of boundless and unconditional cultural self-determination results in the (inevitable but unconfessed) prevalence of the ideological potency of family over all other socialisation mechanisms (school, church, etc.)—namely, the privilege of parents to impose their own ideals and values on their children without outside intervention. One example suffices: in consistent multiculturalism (in which all cultural choices are a priori equally respected), Jehovah's Witnesses would be entitled to decline

not only for themselves, but also for their children, blood transfusions and organ donations. The possibility of conflict between the (relative) popularity of opposing socialisation processes is obviously nothing new (See, for example, Helmut Schelsky, *Schule und Erziehung in der industriellen Gesellschaft* (Würzburg: Werkbund-Verlag, 1957)). It is just that for the first time the proposed solution is based on the principle of favouring individual cultural self-determination *over* public socialisation mechanisms.

19. In this sense, the issue of multiculturalism is purely political. It can be summed up in the political and ideological rejection of the heretofore accepted single-culture prescription, namely the admittance that cultural practices should be exempt from symbolic violence that accompany their official national historical versions. The question of *what* is culture remains, of course, open. At this point it is not possible to provide anything more than vague answers. Even if cultural self-determination explicitly refers to the free choice of the historically and logically open idea of cultural identity, there cannot be clear rational criteria that could help distinguish between cultural identity and political or financial identity (See Amy Gutmann's "Introduction" to Charles Taylor et al., Amy Gutmann (ed.), *Multiculturalism: Examining the Politics of Recognition* (Princeton: Princeton University Press: 1994). In other words, the conceptual separation between political, economic, and cultural spheres is not

but a (historically contingent) *rhematic event.* As Karl Polanyi mentioned, the separation of economy from society was imposed by capitalism precisely because financial practices have always been embedded in social practices. Something similar seems to be underway today in the case of deracinating culture.

20. It is obviously not the covering up of faces that is the issue at hand here, since it is allowed in cases such as motorcycle helmets or costume masks.

21. On this issue, see Giorgio Agamben, *State of Exception,* trans. Kevin Attell (Chicago: University of Chicago Press, 2005)

22. See Paul Ricœur, *Lectures, 1: Autour du politique* (Paris: Seuil, 1991), 308.

23. See Jacques Rancière, *La Haine de la démocratie* (Paris: La Fabrique, 2005), 62–63.

Chapter 6

1. We should remember that during WWII, Lord Beveridge proclaimed the emergence of a new, fairer society that would prioritise full-time employment for the entire body politic.

2. The historical reversal of words and their normative connotation is unremarkable. Until recently, preparation for life—that is to say, the procedures of socialisation—took place once and for all, and incorporation into society appeared conclusive and permanent, while today the use of the terms is diametrically reversed:

the forms of social and labour incorporation of people take place with conclusive processes, and their preparation and socialisation are lifelong and constant.

3. These observations are not only reflected in the recent fetishisation of so-called lifelong learning; they are also expressed in the transformation of the entire philosophy behind education in advanced countries. Currently, the mechanisms of educational reproduction are not as much geared towards ingraining a finite body of knowledge, values, and common cultural prescriptions, as they are towards providing as wide and varied a set of competitive skills as possible. This more or less sums up the pluralistic modernisation of education systems. And on this basis we can interpret the full-fledged weakening of demands for democratisation of education that were dominant in the 1960s and 1970s. Amongst an extensive and significant bibliography, see Pierre Bourdieu and Jean-Claude Passeron, *Les Héritiers: Les étudiants et la culture* (Paris: Minuit, 1964) and *La Reproduction: Éléments pour une théorie du système d'enseignement* (Paris: Minuit, 1970). In our times, the discourse has changed dramatically. The heretofore major issue concerning the class character of educational choice seems to be literally disappearing in favour of promoting the importance of individual responsibility.

4. This is the locus of one of the most significant ideological and political consequences of class-ridden mechanisms of reproduction. Whilst *conclusive educa-*

tion seemed to directly confirm class divisions through the final and lifelong incorporation of the labour force into largely inherited professional hierarchies, *lifelong learning* seems to be transgressing all stable social and ideological dividers through the fictitious redistribution of educational and professional opportunities. This is, of course, a fiction. In reality, class relations (together with the hereditary character of property) are very much reproduced. Combined, the institutional opening up of educational mechanisms to children of lower social classes, and lifelong learning distract our attention from class-ridden educational unfairness.

5. Individual acquisition of knowledge and skills, in order that the latter function as irreproachable normative models must, at least at the imaginary level, appear as detached from class prerequisites as possible. It is not surprising that educational mechanisms will henceforth not appear to be reproducing prescribed social hierarchies, but creating them from scratch based on objectively meritocratic principles. And, in these terms, obvious social mechanisms that confine people to their inherited social class must not be recognised. For the issue of the structure of this confinement, see Daniel Bertaux, *Destins personnels et structure de classe: Pour une critique de l'anthroponomie politique* (Paris: PUF, 1977). The creative role of education appears emancipated and 'upgraded'.

6. See Johan Huizinga, *Homo ludens: Essai sur la fonction sociale du jeu* (Paris: Gallimard, 1951), 81.

7. This terminology was coined by Roger Caillois in *Les Jeux et les hommes: Le masque et le vertige* (Paris: Gallimard, 1958), 9.

8. It is indicative that the widespread social knowledge that since the times of hunters-gatherers contributes to productive processes is not even termed *productive!* In a capitalist world, whatever is not registered as property and does not produce individual rights remains uninteresting and unnamed. The age-old know-how of Bangladeshi farmers, for example, is recognised as a commodity only from the moment that it is registered in the form of intellectual property by multinationals that patent it.

9. In this context, together with the acquisition of *usefulness*, the acquisition of knowledge itself is also transformed. To the degree that the value of individual knowledge is related to its market price, all idealistic representations that insisted on the intrinsic value of knowledge evaporate into thin air. In the place of primary knowledge which concerned the sacrosanct, eternal, and inalienable body of *pure* knowledge, we get the so-called *secondary* function of knowledge which is aimed at maximising the ability of man to *learn to learn*. (See, for example, Gregory Bateson, *Steps to an Ecology of Mind* (New York: Ballantyne, 1972), 140). Or, even, what we might call *tertiary* knowledge, that is a form of strategic un-learning of those remnants of knowledge that seem unusable and unprofitable. If, then, man is a machine that learns, he must also train himself to be

a machine that can forget and selectively dispose of the informational waste that he no longer needs. (See Zygmunt Bauman, *The Individualized Society* (Cambridge: Polity Press, 2001), 123). It is obvious that before we can pose the questions of what constitutes knowledge and what is thought, we must ask ourselves about the way we think about knowledge and thought—and why so. See Clifford Geertz, "The Way We Think Now: Toward an Ethnography of Modern Thought" in *Local Knowledge: Further Essays in Interpretive Anthropology* (New York: Basic Books, 1983), 152.

10. See Jean Baudrillard, *L'Échange impossible* (Paris: Galilée, 1999), 72.

11. See Géza Róheim, *Psychanalyse et anthropologie* (Paris: Gallimard, 1967), 450–457.

12. See Paul Ricœur, *La Mémoire, l'Histoire, l'Oubli* (Paris: Seuil, 1993), 511.

13. Opinions on this matter are obviously divided. See, for example, Mary Thorpe, Richard Edwards, and Ann Hanson (eds.), *Culture and Processes in Adult Learning: A Reader* (London & New York: Routledge, 1987).

14. Borges's *The Lottery in Babylon* describes a society that is based on chance. A covert, out-of this-world, and perhaps superintelligent Company performs draws that determine the revocable and temporary fate of all people. "Like all men in Babylon I have been a proconsul; like all, a slave": this impossible society is no more than a metaphysical play. Being logically perfect,

however, it seems completely acceptable. If someone is not responsible for their own fate, they can distance themselves from it, accept it, and wait until it changes.

15. The tendency to replace social provisions and the social rights that legitimised them with *safety networks* that embody the absolute minimum of survival is typical of our times. The inalienable right of access to the principal goods of civilisation is replaced by the institution of assistance for the unfortunate—available only *in extremis*.

16. Based on the classic anthropological distinction between cultures of shame and cultures of guilt, we could argue that the postmodern era achieved an effective composition between those two forms of social control. From the moment that, distorted through the gaze of others, individual success and failure are perceived as the combination of personal causal factors, the Aristotelian proverb that *shame dwells in the eyes* and the Judaeo-Christian internalisation of sin can coincide and overlap. The undeserving are ashamed because they are guilty; and act as guilty because of their shame.

17. It is not surprising to observe that, for the first time in history, free man is called on to negotiate, rationally and for himself, all the perils that could befall him. This might have been justified while the enormous financial burden was still being paid for by the widening social state. But from the moment that individuals become answerable for the cost of their actions,

repression of self-destructive acts can only be justified by fetishising utilitarian rationalism. People nowadays are expected to live as rational, prudent, healthy, and vigorous rational agents within a newfangled system of transgressions and stigmas that is instituted in the name of a globally effective and rationally instrumental rhetoric. In these terms, the conscious choice of unacceptable risk-taking appears tantamount to choosing repulsive misery. Stubbornly resisting multicultural tolerance, the rational panoptical biopolitical power fetishises the cultivation of a new instrumental ideological homogenisation. In the name of self-preservative rationalism, new political alliances will be forged. And, obviously, this is only the beginning. (See Gilles Deleuze, "Postface", in Jacques Donzelot, *La Police des familles* (Paris: Minuit, 1977), 216).

18. Suffice it to say that the impairment of public responsibility for the welfare of individuals weakens the symbolic and material *duties* that individuals assume towards the community. (For this issue, see Gilles Lipovetsky, *Le Crépuscule du devoir* (Paris: Gallimard, 1992).

19. This topic concerned the later Michel Foucault.

20. Michel Foucault, *The Archaeology of Knowledge* (New York: Pantheon Books, 1972), 131.

21. See Richard Sennett, *The Culture of the New Capitalism* (New Haven: Yale University Press, 2006).

22. See Guy Debord, *The Society of the Spectacle* (New York: Zone Books, 1995).

23. Alfred Jarry, "Ubu Enchained", in *The Ubu Plays* (New York: Grove Press, 1968), 110.

Chapter 7

1. Claude Lévi-Strauss *Tristes tropiques* (Paris: Plon, 1955), 101.

2. See Richard Rorty, "Is 'Cultural Recognition' a Useful Concept for Leftist Politics?", in Christopher J. Voparil and Richard J. Bernstein (eds.), *The Rorty Reader* (Oxford: Wiley-Blackwell, 2010), 463 f. See also Todd Gitlin, "From Universality to Difference: Notes on the Fragmentation of the Idea of the Left", in Craig Calhoun (ed.), *Social Theory and the Politics of Identity* (Oxford: Blackwell, 1994), 150.

3. Although the social strata militant minds come from says nothing about the normative validity or the effectiveness of their claims, it remains indicative of the social reality within which they emerge.

4. Giorgio Agamben, *Moyens sans fin: Notes sur la politique* (Paris: Payot-Rivages, 2002). See also Zygmunt Bauman, *Identité* (Paris: L'Herne, 2010), 56. Also notable is the argument proposed by some liberals, such as Walzer, who claim that by voluntarily moving, these people accept the consequences of their incorporation into the host society. (See Michael Walzer in Charles Taylor et al., Amy Gutmann (ed.), *Multiculturalism: Examining the Politics of Recognition* (Princeton: Princeton University Press: 1994), 102–103).

5. See Zygmunt Bauman, *Identité* (Paris: L'Herne, 2010), 57–58.

6. Jacques Derrida, "Points de suspension", in *Points…: Interviews, 1974–1994*, ed. E. Weber (Stanford: Stanford University Press, 1995), 277.

7. See Jürgen Habermas, *Le Discours philosophique de la modernité: Douze conférences* (Paris: Gallimard, 1988), IX–X.

8. Michel de Certeau, *La Culture au pluriel* (Paris: Seuil, 1993), 168.

9. See Slavoj Žižek's interview to Γιάννης Σταυρακάκης in Slavoj Žižek, *Το υψηλό αντικείμενο της ιδεολογίας,* trans. Βίκυ Ιακώβου and ed. Γιάννης Σταυρακάκης (Athens: Scripta, 2006), 400–401.

10. Theodor W. Adorno, "Aphorism 94", in *Minima Moralia*, trans. Dennis Redmond, 2005.

11. See Claude Lévi-Strauss, "Introduction a l'œuvre de Marcel Mauss", in Marcel Mauss, *Sociologie et anthropologie* (Paris: PUF, 1960), XXXVIII.

12. This is the reason why, ninety years after its publication, Marcel Mauss's *The Gift* continues to provoke debates across the humanities.

13. See, for example, Georges Bataille, *La Part maudite* (Paris: Minuit, 1967).

14. See Albert O. Hirschman, *The Passions and the Interests: Political Arguments for Capitalism Before its Triumph* (Princeton: Princeton University Press, 1977).

15. According to Sir Henry Maine in his classic *Ancient Law*.

16. Although they didn't entirely disappear, gifts and symbolic exchanges are nowadays regulated in the context of hybrid *unbalanced agreements* that constrict their reach and trivialise their social significance. Even more, rational transactional regulations consider gifts to be inherent anomalies. On this issue, see Κωνσταντίνος Τσουκαλάς, *Είδωλα πολιτισμού: Ελευθερία, ισότητα και αδελφότητα στη σύγχρονη πολιτεία* (Αθήνα: Θεμέλιο, 1998).

17. We can see here the normative absurdity underlying the need for reciprocity of social security. Indeed, this idea does nothing else but conventionalise the values of social clemency and solidarity, subsuming them in a temporally antecedent—therefore quantifiable—compliance with financial criteria and conditions. And, in this sense, the fundamental moral dimension of social cohesion seems to be dictated by undisguised financial criteria, and public social security is expected to function in the same logic as private insurance. From the moment that the widely accepted *do ut des* sets the terms of social security and solidarity, the moral constitution of society is perceived only under the condition that individualistic rationalism will be religiously observed. Before it is elevated into an organisational, technical, and financial necessity, the idea of reciprocity appears as a momentous reversal. The idea of social cohesion and solidarity is absolved of its eternal symbolic implications and is brought under the rule of a widespread financial logic.

In reality, this is a major campaign to transfer moral responsibility away from the barely surviving state-as-shepherd. The redistributed funds do not come from society as a whole but from specific organisations that are asked to collect and, if necessary, reclaim (!) the individual contributions of citizens. The rational circle is, thus, squared through the full privatisation of social security.

18. See Jacques Derrida, *Donner le temps: 1. La fausse monnaie* (Paris: Galilée, 1991), 57–59.

19. Twenty years before Fukuyama's end of history, the organised European corporatism was priding itself on having discovered the universal cure for a self-reproducing and fairly distributed harmony.

20. This has been thoroughly analysed in Κωνσταντίνος Τσουκαλάς, *Είδωλα πολιτισμού: Ελευθερία, ισότητα και αδελφότητα στη σύγχρονη πολιτεία* (Αθήνα: Θεμέλιο, 1998).

21. Here we can also mention the widespread moralisation of private political behaviours which occurs via the fetishisation of societies, the excessive encouragement of the principles of voluntarism (which has to take place outside, regardless, and maybe juxtaposed to survival through work—like, for example, the American Nobelist Robert Fogel proposes in *The Fourth Great Awakening and the Future of Egalitarianism* (Chicago & London: University of Chicago Press, 2000)), sponsorship and personal charity and, in a general sense, the emergence of the so-called

post-materialistic culture (see Ronald Inglehart, *Culture Shift in Advanced Industrial Society* (Princeton: Princeton University Press, 1990)). The common denominator of all these pseudo-innovative projects is the need to install private enterprise in the place of the traditional functions of the social whole; in other words, to compensate for the gaps and malfunctions of the public space through the private arena. "Left alone, the world of promiscuous speculative profiteering is the best possible one". (See Κωνσταντίνος Τσουκαλάς, "Η Κοινωνία των πολιτών ως 'χώρος ελευθερίας': Πολιτικές αναγνώσεις μιας μυθοπλασίας", in Μαρία Κούση, Μηνάς Σαματάς and Σωκράτης Κονιόρδος, *Εξουσία και κοινωνία: Δωρήματα στον Κωνσταντίνο Τσουκαλά* (Αθηνα: Κασταντιώτης, 2010), 429).

22. See Gregory Bateson, *Steps to an Ecology of Mind* (New York: Ballantyne, 1972), 243.

23. See Fred Hirsch, *Social Limits to Growth* (London: Routledge & Kegan Paul, 1977).

24. See Carl Schmitt, *Political Romanticism* (Cambridge, MA: The MIT Press, 1986), 7.

25. I owe this observation to George Krimbas.

26. T. S. Elliot, *The Cocktail Party*, Act I, Scene III, (London: Faber, 1976), 65.

27. Jean-Jacques Rousseau, "Discours sur l'origine de l'inégalité parmi les hommes", in *Du contrat social* (Paris: U.G.E., 1973), 382.

28. See the works of René Girard.

29. Only under this condition is it possible to under-

stand the principles of justice described by John Rawls. The demand for redistribution of social benefits and handicaps is based on the principle that the main aim of justice is to minimise handicaps for the less privileged groups (John Rawls, *A Theory of Justice*). Even if these defects are reflected on the symbolic and ideological plane, they are primarily material. Tolerance and recognition could never cure the ignominy of starvation.

30. All attempted distinctions between nominal and actual freedom, between genuine and insincere needs and desires, between real and fake consciousness, and between a self that is really free and one that is ideologically manipulated are substantiated on this claim. Obviously, these are false dilemmas. By definition, all aspects of free consciousness cannot be but the results of a contingent and cunning history. The only thing that makes our times different is not related to the historicity itself of these phenomena. Rather, it can be found in the fact that supposedly historical ideas about freedom, necessity, and individual identity are uncoupled from their objective specifications and are considered to be the results of free choice. (See Fredric Jameson, *Archaeologies of the Future: The Desire Called Utopia and Other Science Fictions* (London & New York: Verso, 2005), 142).

31. See Paul Ricœur, "Tolérance, Intolérance, Intolérable", in *Lectures, 1: Autour du politique* (Paris: Seuil, 1991), 200.

32. Since Bernard Madeville described the market

as an invention that *turns private perversions into public benefit*, the dominant thought did not stop trying to disengage self-interest from its perverse preconditions.

33. Arjun Appadurai, *Modernity at Large: Cultural Dimensions of Globalization* (Minneapolis: University of Minnesota Press, 1996).

34. See, amongst others, Jutta Weldes et al., *Cultures of Insecurity: States, Communities, and the Production of Danger* (Minncapolis: University of Minnesota Press, 1999).

35. Anna Akhmatova, "Requiem", in Roberta Reeder (ed.), Judith Hemschemeyer (trans.), *The Complete Poems of Anna Akhmatova* (Somerville: Zephyr Press, 2000).

CONSTANTINE
TSOUCALAS'S
AGE OF ANXIETY
WAS PRINTED
IN LONDON IN
SEPTEMBER 2018
SET IN BODONI